Capital City

The Jacobin series includes short interrogations of politics, economics, and culture from a socialist perspective, as an avenue to radical political practice. The books offer critical analysis and engagement with the history and ideas of the Left in accessible and popular form.

The series is a collaboration between Verso Books and *Jacobin* magazine, which is published quarterly in print and online at jacobinmag.com.

Capital City

Gentrification and the
Real Estate State

SAMUEL STEIN

VERSO
London · New York

First published by Verso 2019
© Samuel Stein 2019

5 7 9 10 8 6 4

Verso
UK: 6 Meard Street, London W1F 0EG
US: 20 Jay Street, Suite 1010, Brooklyn, NY 11201
www.versobooks.com

Verso is the imprint of New Left Books

ISBN-13: 978-1-78663-639-3
ISBN-13: 978-1-78663-637-9 (UK EBK)
ISBN-13: 978-1-78663-638-6 (US EBK)

British Library Cataloguing in Publication Data
A catalogue record for this book is available from the British Library

Library of Congress Cataloging-in-Publication Data
A catalog record for this book is available from the Library of Congress

Typeset in Monotype Fournier
Printed and bound by CPI Group (UK) Ltd, Croydon, CR0 4YY

Contents

For my father, Joshua B. Stein (1944–2012),
who taught me to love cities and question authorities.

Introduction

On March 25, 1911, fire engulfed New York's Triangle Shirt-waist Factory. The bosses had locked the doors and 146 workers were killed. Two days later, the Jewish socialist newspaper *The Forward* printed an impassioned plea from its editor, Abraham Cahan. After describing the pain felt throughout Manhattan's Lower East Side, Cahan wrote that mourners were beginning to see a figure through their tears: the biblical Angel of Death. "Who is the Angel of Death? Who is the thug? Who is the mass murderer? Must we again say it is that gluttonous ravager of humans—capital?!"[1]

Just over a century later, a public housing complex in West London called the Grenfell Tower burst into flames. Though residents had warned that the building was a firetrap, public

---

In order to keep the price of this book low, the publisher and I have agreed to reduce the number of citations in the print edition. For a fully cited version, please see the book's electronic format.

1   Cahan, Abraham. "The blood of the victims calls to us." *Forverts* [*The Forward*], March 27, 1911.

authorities allowed it to deteriorate. When the fire started, it quickly accelerated due to the highly flammable cladding that management had added to the building's exterior in order to make it more attractive to posh neighbors. The fire killed over seventy tenants.

Who is the Angel of Death? Who is the mass murderer? Today, as a century ago, the culprit is capital, rushing in and out of spaces with abandon in search of profit and growth. In 1911, the arsonist was industrial capital, then the dominant force in urban politics. In 2017, it was real estate capital.

Around the world, more and more money is being invested in real estate, the business of building, buying and renting land and property. You can sense it as you walk through most cities, and feel it every time you pay the rent or mortgage.

Global real estate is now worth $217 trillion, thirty-six times the value of all the gold ever mined.[2] It makes up 60 percent of the world's assets, and the vast majority of that wealth— roughly 75 percent—is in housing.[3] There are a number of reasons why capital is converging on land and buildings: a long period of financial deregulation, low federal interest rates and "quantitative easing" in the United States; massive urbanization programs in China, the United Arab Emirates and several other countries; a proliferation of predatory equity funds scouring the globe for "undervalued" investment

---

2   Farha, Leilani. "Report of the Special Rapporteur on adequate housing as a component of the right to an adequate standard of living, and on the right to non-discrimination in this context." *United Nations Human Rights Council*, January 18, 2017.

3   Ibid.

opportunities and finding them in housing; economic polarization around the world, with extremely wealthy and somewhat nervous individuals viewing property as the safest place to hide their money; and more. When capital gains rise while rates of profit plummet across many once-dynamic sectors of the economy, real estate becomes the latest stop on what geographer Cindi Katz calls "vagabond" capitalism's eternal search for profitability.[4]

In the United States, homes are changing hands at a rapid pace, but homeownership is at a fifty-year low. In 2016, a record 37 percent of home sales were made to absentee investors.[5] While some of those buyers were pensionless seniors who needed a retirement strategy, most of them were banks, hedge funds and private equity firms like Blackstone—now the world's largest landlord.

As renting rises, so do rents. Average move-in rents in the United States have more than doubled over the last two decades.[6] Prices vary dramatically across the country, but the trend is clearly upward, with the fastest growth in mid-sized cities like Seattle, Portland, Denver and Cincinnati. Wages, however, remain stagnant, putting tenants in a bind. There is not a single county in the country where a full-time minimum

---

4   Katz, Cindi. "Vagabond capitalism and the necessity of social reproduction." *Antipode* 33.4 (2001): 709–28; Rapoza, Kenneth. "Why the best investment in 2016 might be global real estate." *Forbes*, January 5, 2016.

5   Clark, Patrick. "Landlords are taking over the US housing market." *Bloomberg*, February 23, 2017.

6   US Census Bureau. *Housing Vacancies and Homeownership (CPS/HVS)*. Table 11A/B: "Quarterly median asking rent and sales prices of the US and Regions: 1988 to present." 2018.

wage worker can afford the average two-bedroom apartment.[7]
Rent burdens—the percentage of income tenants put toward
housing—are becoming oppressive, particularly for people
of color in segregated neighborhoods. Around the country,
rent burdens in Black neighborhoods average 44 percent; in
Latino neighborhoods, it's 48 percent.[8] Every month in New
York City, almost two million people pass most of their income
to landlords.[9]

With wages flat, many people—even those with full-time
jobs—simply cannot afford stable housing. Last year, as cities and states continued to pass punitive legislation against the
poor, about 2 million people in the United States went homeless
and 7 million more lived in precarious housing situations—
doubled or tripled up, couch surfing or sleeping in shift beds.[10]
This opens the door to an entire industry of private homeless
services, with philanthropic and real estate capital blended to
find profits in extreme poverty.

The force behind these trends is the growing centrality of
urban real estate to capital's global growth strategy. Through
this process, the price of land becomes a central economic
determinate and a dominant political issue. The clunky term

7   Aurand, Andrew, Dan Emmanuel, Diane Yentel, Ellen Errico, Jared
Gaby-Biegel and Emma Kerr. *Out of Reach 2018: The High Cost of Housing.*
National Low Income Housing Coalition, 2018.

8   Kurtz, Annalyn. "Black and Hispanic communities are spending almost
half their incomes on rent." *Fortune*, March 29, 2017.

9   NYU Furman Center. *State of New York City Housing and Neighborhoods
in 2015.* 2016.

10   Gee, Alastair, Liz Barney and Julia O'Malley. "Outside in America:
How America counts its homeless—and why so many are overlooked." *The
Guardian*, February 16, 2017.

"gentrification" becomes a household word and displacement an everyday fact of life. Housing becomes a globally traded financial asset, creating the conditions for synchronized bubbles and crashes. Government, particularly at the municipal level, becomes increasingly obsessed with raising property values and redistributing wealth upward through land and rents. Real estate developer Donald Trump becomes first a celebrity and ultimately a president. Taken together, we witness the rise of the *real estate state*, a political formation in which real estate capital has inordinate influence over the shape of our cities, the parameters of our politics and the lives we lead.

The real estate state is not new, nor is it all-encompassing. Like the carceral state, the warfare state, the welfare state or the administrative state, it is an expression of government—a component, a bloc, a manifestation, a tendency—that has been around in one form or another for as long as states and private property have existed. Landowners have been determining the shape of cities for centuries, and the idea of housing as a commodity—even as a financial asset—is not exactly state of the art. What is relatively new, however, is the outsized power of real estate interests within the capitalist state. As real estate values have risen to absurd heights, so has the political force of real estate capital.

The real estate state is a feature of government at all levels, from the hyper-local to the global. It is most firmly grafted onto municipal governments, however, because that is where much of the capitalist state's physical planning is done. City planners therefore sit uncomfortably at the center of this maelstrom. Planners manage the levers of urban change and make crucial decisions about land use, transportation, housing, the environment and more. Though most people have no idea what they actually do, planners have an immense impact on both capitalists and workers in cities and suburbs. In most places, planners are tasked with the contradictory goals of inflating real estate values while safeguarding residents' best interests. Capitalism never made planning easy—organized money could always thwart the best laid plans—but today's urban planners face an existential crisis: if the city is an investment strategy, are they just wealth managers?

This book is about planners in cities run by real estate. It describes how real estate came to rule, and what planners do under these circumstances. Planners provide a window into the practical dynamics of urban change: the way the state both uses and is used by organized capital, and the power of landlords and developers at every level of government. They also possess some of the powers we must deploy if we ever wish to reclaim our cities from real estate capital. Understanding planners is an important way to understand the capitalist state—how it is built, and what it would take to dismantle it.

While the nexus of planning and real estate is a powerful dynamic in nearly every city, I mostly focus on the United States, and often use New York City as a prime example. I realize there is some risk in focusing on New York: for a US city, it is exceptionally large, dense and expensive. But as the biggest city in the United States, it serves as an example for many other places. Planners from around the country look to New York for new patterns and practices. It is also a place where real estate's rule is clearly seen and deeply felt. The rents are outrageous, and the cost of living is among the most persistent public issues. Most of all, though, I use New York because it is my home and the place from which I see the world. I know its gridded streets as well as its crooked politicians, and I've lived here long enough to feel like the city knows me too.

I am a planner. Though I don't work for a government agency and I'm not in charge of managing any physical spaces, I was trained as a planner and I maintain elements of the planner's worldview: to be simultaneously abstract and concrete, utopian and pragmatic; to imagine what doesn't yet exist while figuring out how to get there; to care about systems and processes, the way things work and the way they ought to. Fundamentally, we believe it is a good idea to have a plan—an explication of the future. Planning is a way of knowing the world as well as a way of remaking it.

Like a lot of people, I became interested in planning because I was mad at planners. I loved my city, but I hated what it was becoming. I came to know New York at the start of the twenty-first century, when it seemed like construction cranes were as common as pigeons and scaffolding was the new streetscape. Gigantic glass towers were rising all over the place, reflecting the old city grotesquely through their distorted mirror facades.

I thought the architecture was stupid, but that wasn't what really bothered me. I was working for a union, and though we were winning big victories, there was a growing sense that the city we were fighting for was disappearing all around us. The working class people who made the city could no longer afford to live in it. Rents were skyrocketing and culturally important spaces were shuttering. I learned the rent laws' limits when

I was kicked out of a low-cost apartment. It was a stark lesson in landlord-tenant power relations: my landlord tried to kill the downstairs neighbors and torch the place, but he got to keep the building; the lessee had sublet the apartment to me without registering and we were served an eviction notice.

I was excited by some endeavors that New York City planners were undertaking at the time, like building public plazas and extending the bike network, but I knew these benefits were linked to larger plots: rezonings that brought luxury development; mega-projects that turned the urban fabric threadbare; and management schemes that turned public goods into private fiefdoms. I pursued planning because I wanted to understand how the city works, and to figure out how to preserve the best parts and change the worst. I believed in planning's promise of better spaces and a better society, even if I understood intuitively that planners had not exactly delivered on it. I had two basic questions: First, how much planning will capitalism allow in market-based systems? And second, how can we improve our cities without inducing gentrification and displacement?

I spent two and a half years studying planning history and theory, quantitative and qualitative methods, public finance, transportation, housing and more. I learned a little about planning, and a lot more about how planners think. There were tons of good ideas bandied about, and countless practical ways to reapportion space and rethink urban infrastructures. But I had a hard time answering my questions.

It seemed like the system allowed quite a bit of planning intervention when it benefited business, including massive infrastructure projects and tax incentives for development, but it imposed strict limitations on planners who aimed to alter the balance of power. These limits are especially hard drawn when it comes to private property and real estate, which meant answering my second question—how can we improve cities without sparking displacement?—wasn't going to be easy, either. There appeared to be a close link between "good planning" and gentrification, since private property owners could capitalize on the value the state adds to land. By the end of my education, I realized that capitalism makes the best of planning impossible: any good that planners do is filtered through a system that dispossesses those who cannot pay.

Planning today is defined by incredible dreams and stultifying realities. A planner's mission is to imagine a better world, but their day-to-day work involves producing a more profitable one. They almost universally espouse a commitment to pluralism and diversity, but the profession is 58 percent male and 81 percent White—demographics that are way out of step with the residents of the cities where most planners work.[11] Though most planning offices are structured to build continuity across changing administrations, planners are still beholden to politicians and their political appointees. Their agendas almost always tend to favor their most powerful supporters—a group that usually includes some strain of real estate capital. And while planning is a public function, planners in capitalist cities are always at the mercy of the market, since most of what they do is regulate private actions. The money

---

11   American Planning Association. *APA/AICP planners salary survey: Planner characteristics.* 2016.

planners have to work with is largely derived from property taxes, an arrangement that incentivizes developer and home-owner-friendly policies, and restricts the amount of land that is given over to truly public uses.

A private land market is essentially a spoils system—whoever owns the land keeps the accrued benefits, whether or not the owner is responsible for them. Until land is socially controlled, those who possess property, capital and access to power will shape planning priorities. With so much global capital invested into real estate, planners are facing enormous pressure to stoke land markets and enable gentrification. Their charge is to find creative ways to raise property values—either because they are low and landowners want them higher, or because they are already high and city budgets will fail if they start to fall. Any seemingly technical discussions of growth, density or urban form are always also shaped by this imperative. Planners are not just shills to real estate, though; they can and generally want to make spaces more beautiful, sustainable, efficient and sociable. But without control over the land, the result of their work is often higher land prices, increased rents and ultimately displacement.

As some places endure this kind of land market inflation, others fall prey to disinvestment: their land loses its exchange value, their residents are shut out of credit markets and their buildings fall into dangerous disrepair. This leads to a land-scape of radically uneven geographical development between capital-flush cosmopolitan centers, like New York and Lon-don, and investment-scarce cities like Camden, New Jersey and Blackpool on England's Irish Sea coast. Even within cities, the same inequalities are often evident from neighborhood to neighborhood. Gentrification cannot be a universal phenomenon; money tends to come from one place and go to another, creating chaos on both ends. On the disinvested side, communities face terrible choices. Many want the benefits of good planning—safe streets, clean air, decent housing—but not the catastrophic tide of capital it summons. In these places, residents will often reject planners' interventions out of a well-founded fear that they will be kicked out of their neighborhoods before they ever enjoy the promised improvements.

One recent example: in March 2017, New York State Governor Andrew Cuomo announced a major new initiative for the poorest parts of Brooklyn. The plan promised jobs, parks, health care and housing at a cost of $1.4 billion. But Brownsville resident Dayon Hopkins was skeptical. He had already been displaced from Bedford Stuyvesant after that neighborhood started to gentrify. Pointing to an ordinary building, he told a *New York Times* reporter, "They'll take this right here, and put a glass door, a brick wall on one side of the hallway, and now it's a loft, and now it costs way more than people are making around these parts. And I understand: It does get nicer. But where's everybody else going to go? Down south? Where are we going to go?'"[12]

Hopkins says what most planners won't: that as long as some people's business is to profit off land and property, most people will not be able to enjoy the benefits planners promise. Of

---

12   Maslin Nir, Sarah. "Cuomo's $1.4 billion plan for Brooklyn stirs fears of gentrification." *New York Times*, March 14, 2017.

course, it doesn't have to be this way. We can imagine a better world—in fact, we must. First, however, we need to understand how we got here and how the system works.

I wrote this book for anyone who is frustrated with both the direction their cities are taking and the alternatives planners are offering. I put planners at the center of the story because they are uniquely positioned at the nexus of state, capital and popular power. On their own, however, planners cannot unwind real estate's grip over our politics. For that, we will need organized people: mass movements to remake our cities from the ground up, and gain control over our homes and lives.

Such movements have been a consistent feature of urban life, and have grown and adapted to face new challenges. Gentrification is brutal, but rarely total—not only because colonizers always rely on the labor of a local workforce, but also because people always fight back: as individuals, as families (of birth and of choice), as communities (local and international), as neighbors and as a class. Even after displacement, people find a way to remake their spatial cultures and rebuild their social ties—not just to survive, but to fight back anew.

Gentrification's apologists will see this and claim displacement is not that bad—people are resilient, they move, they rebuild, they're fine. My point is precisely the opposite: human beings will always resist regimes in which land ownership gives a small number of people enormous power over the lives of all others. People will fight back, and I believe that we will win. I hope this book contributes to that fight. It is made not only to be read, but to be used.

1

The Rise of the Real Estate State

What is planning?
What exactly do planners do?

Planning is the way we shape space over time. In geographer Ruth Wilson Gilmore's terms, the point of planning is "to have some sense of how to secure the future."[1] It happens on multiple scales: individuals plan for their own survival and advancement; households plan ways to make their incomes stretch and their futures brighter; businesses plan in highly structured and rigorous ways, creating schemes to eclipse the competition and increase their profitability; communities and movements plan strategies for survival and resistance, and produce "insurgent" plans that chart the way from deprivation to freedom.

Often, however, what we talk about when we talk about planning is government. For more than a century, professional planners have been a crucial element of the state, and have made important decisions about the ways our cities and towns function. In the United States, planners are usually municipal

---

1   Gilmore, Ruth Wilson. *Golden gulag: Prisons, surplus, crisis, and opposition in globalizing California*. University of California Press, 2007, 175.

employees, but they work in all levels of government and include outside actors—consultants, designers, nonprofits and so on—who seek to influence land use decisions. They survey and map the physical and cultural landscape, plot what can go where and at what size and shape, design infrastructure systems to move people and products, and channel investment and development toward certain places and away from others.

The nature of planning in capitalist democracies like the United States is mercurial and contradictory. No city is entirely planned, but none is devoid of planning. Our political discourse valorizes the free market in a way that makes planning seem unnecessary, yet the United States has consistently regulated its urban spaces in important and powerful ways. Americans often think of planners as either bureaucratic cogs or totalitarian tyrants, but planners tend to see themselves as promoters of fairness and protectors of the common good.

Throughout the profession's history, planners have enacted a pair of opposing tendencies: a pragmatic utopianism, which aims to bring about a new world from the structures (if not the ashes) of the old; and a crude commitment to capital, which divides space by race and seeks ever newer frontiers for private development. US planners are committed to both securing social reproduction—or ensuring that people have the means to survive into the future—and to turning everyone's space into someone's profit. They are motivated by the social movements that animate history, as well as by the economic powers that structure political realities. This assures that the beauty of urban planning is always accompanied by its horrors. In the words of planning scholar Ananya Roy, "planning's promise of creation and creativity is not possible without a frontier of destruction."[2]

The Rise of Professional Planning

The practice of planning is as old as human settlement, and in the United States it reflects all the conflicts and contradictions of this country's history. Indigenous nations planned both stable settlements and migratory villages throughout the Americas, which included residential and commercial areas as well as open spaces and commons. In a spatial form of primitive accumulation, European imperialists and settler colonists built on these plans and often superimposed their street grids over existing native trails. By 1573, the Spanish Crown published their *Orders of Discovery, New Settlements and Pacification*, which codified decades of colonial town planning practice into a set of strict standards for spatial segregation, ordered development and efficient extraction. Planning scholar Clyde Woods argues that the United States' first real plan was for "the total elimination, marginalization, or exile of indigenous people."[3] Proto-planners enabled the country's murderous westward expansion, and mapped the rail networks and other infrastructure that made it possible.

The plantations that eventually dotted and dominated the southern landscape were a highly planned built form, which

---

2   Roy, Ananya. "Praxis in the time of empire." *Planning Theory* 5.1 (2006): 7–29.

3   Woods, Clyde Adrian. *Development arrested: The blues and plantation power in the Mississippi Delta*. Verso, 1998, 41.

in turn created a template for future US urban and suburban development as well as contemporary "factories in the fields." Within the plantation, however, slaves planned their own plots—spaces in which to cultivate their own food and practice everyday acts of resistance. While early town designs were largely imported from European models and reflected Greco-Roman and Enlightenment-era conceptions of order and environmental control, other essential American forms—such as the skinny, rectangular "shotgun house" design common in the south—were derived from longstanding West African architectural practices.

The United States' largest city, New York, was built on Lenape land as a series of scattered settlements emerging from Lower Manhattan. By 1811, city leaders had imposed a rigid street grid pattern and a standardized set of twenty-five-by-one hundred-foot lots, literally paving the way for future real estate development. (The main exception to the grid, Broadway, was superimposed over a preexisting Native American trail.) Long before zoning became common practice throughout the country, New York exerted land use and social controls through fire codes and nuisance laws.

While the *practice* of planning has therefore long been established, the *profession* of planning is a more recent phenomenon. Modern urban planning emerged in Europe and the Americas as a formal art, science and vocation in the mid-nineteenth and early twentieth centuries, a moment of rapid industrial expansion, massive rural-to-urban and international migration, and widespread social, economic and political upheaval. In Europe, the establishment of urban planning followed a series of proletarian uprisings in the major cities of England, France, Germany and beyond. The most famous case is Barron Haussmann's reorientation of Paris. In the mid-nineteenth century, after a series of barricaded rebellions broke out on the city's streets—a form of working class insurrectionary planning—Napoleon III appointed Haussmann to remake Paris' physical layout, driving wide boulevards through the city's neighborhoods and displacing thousands. This reflected not just an aesthetic preference for strong sightlines and harmonious architecture, but the ruling class's desire to defend their hold on the city and prevent more working class uprisings.

In the United States, planning's formalization tracked not only with northern industrialization and the burgeoning labor movement, but also the end of southern reconstruction, which in 1935 sociologist W.E.B Du Bois characterized as "a revolution comparable to the upheavals in France in the past, and in Russia, Spain, India and China today."[4] In cities like Chicago, grand Haussmann-esque plans were drawn up to modernize the city—ironically by imposing neoclassical design aesthetics—and attract real estate and industrial capital. In cities like Birmingham, planners wrote land use codes to simultaneously attract mining investment and suppress Black labor mobility.

In both the European and US cases, the planning profession arose at moments of extreme social contest and turmoil, which were expressed in fights for control over land. It is no coincidence, then, that from its onset, urban planning has contained

---

4   Du Bois, William Edward Burghardt. *Black reconstruction in America: Toward a history of the part which Black folk played in the attempt to reconstruct democracy in America, 1860–1880.* Free Press, 1997 [1935], 708.

both *reformist* strands, which sought to maintain elite control of urban space while smoothing over capitalism's rough spots, and *radical* visions, which imagined planning as a means to overturn the social order and create and maintain a socialist society.

A Brief History of US Urban Planning

Early US planning history is marked less by bold experiments in egalitarian design than systematic attempts to juice urban land markets for private gain. These initial planning impulses were formulated through three interlocking urban movements, each of which left a profound legacy on contemporary planning and city life: *progressive reformism*, *City Beautiful* and *City Practical*.

Progressive reformers tried to reshape the city toward three simultaneous ends: to ensure the social reproduction of a rapidly growing industrial labor force; to quell the urban rebellions that were rocking nineteenth- and early twentieth-century cities; and to boost profits. In some cities, this took the form of "municipal socialism," in which public monopolies took control of infrastructure development and maintenance. In others, progressives developed settlement houses, which provided much-needed social services to poor urban migrants, while also imposing norms of patriarchy and Protestantism. Perhaps the progressive reform movement's most enduring legacy in US cities was imposing building codes, which provided minimum construction standards that promoted health and safety. The New York City tenement laws of 1867, 1879 and 1901, for example, ensured that new residential buildings would have fire escapes, air shafts, windows and toilets. In so doing, these laws managed to simultaneously create somewhat safer housing while driving up property values. The result was that the poorest families could not live in new tenements and were relegated to the least safe and worst maintained properties in the city. Meanwhile, rising land and construction costs centralized new housing development in the hands of a wealthy elite.

"City Beautiful" was perhaps the first self-identified planning movement in the United States, coalescing around the inaugural 1909 National Conference on City Planning and Congestion and setting a high standard for urban design and aesthetics. Before all else, however, City Beautiful was a real estate program that sought to attract investment by building massive, Beaux Arts-inspired municipal buildings, tree-lined boulevards and carefully manicured open spaces. The movement is frequently associated with architect Daniel Burnham, who created the 1909 *Plan of Chicago* before taking his approach to Detroit, Washington, DC, and US-occupied Manila, but its presence is also felt in New York, from the Manhattan Municipal Building to Grand Central Terminal. Inspired in part by Haussmann, City Beautiful projects were often built on centrally located land inhabited by poor people, immigrants and African Americans, who were treated as wholly incompatible with and undeserving of urban beauty. Central Park, for example, was built over the largest Black settlement in Manhattan, Seneca Village, and also displaced large numbers of Irish and German immigrants who were living on coveted real estate.

While local elites desperately wanted a more "beautiful" city, they refused to either pay for these developments or relinquish control over them. The solution, then, was a system of municipal planning with strong "public" input: the city planning commission. Established in most US cities in the first half of the twentieth century, these largely unelected commissions were often populated by real estate elites, who tried to ensure that city planning decisions would stimulate profits. They approved monumental projects—grand boulevards, parks, museums, municipal complexes and more—which resulted in higher urban property values and were largely paid for by the public.

Planning commissions marked the shift from City Beautiful to *City Practical*. During a time when cities were growing chaotically and radical social movements were gaining steam, this less famous but profoundly important movement aimed to formalize and expand the scope of planning in the United States in order to rationalize urban and peri-urban expansion. Though rarely acknowledged, one of the most important forces behind City Practical was archconservative Herbert Hoover, who, as secretary of commerce from 1920 to 1928, oversaw the establishment of the federal Standard State Zoning Enabling Act (SSZEA) and the Standard City Planning Enabling Act (SCPEA). These two laws empowered municipal governments to write "master plans" for their cities, and to create zoning ordinances that mapped out what kinds of buildings (residential, commercial, industrial, etc.) could be built where and at what sizes. While some capitalists bristled at the idea of property controls and master planning, Hoover's Department of Commerce argued that planning was ultimately in their best interest for it helped them predict how both residents and politicians would respond to their proposals, and therefore increased the chances that a conforming project would be supported.

Around the country, many master plans would be produced but few would be strictly implemented. Instead, cities like New York relied on zoning as their primary planning mechanism. Zoning, however, is not just a technical planning technique; as geographer Bobby Wilson argues, "zoning had been developed as a tool for rational land use planning, but it became a tool for accommodating the racial order."[5] In the United States, zoning was always exclusionary. Modesto, California introduced the country's first zoning in 1885 as a way of barring Chinese people from areas of the city. It came to New York in 1916, and among its most vocal proponents were Fifth Avenue's high-end merchants, who lobbied the city to zone out manufacturing in order to keep Jewish garment workers off their streets and away from their customers. The SSZEA and SCPEA gave every city in the United States the power to enact such programs.

With this political infrastructure in place, state planning power grew stronger throughout the country, reaching its apex in the *rational comprehensive planning movement* of the 1940s, '50s and '60s. This movement dovetailed with the massive expansion of state and military capacity involved in the Second World War and its aftermaths, and built on the planning theories and engineering systems that both the Allies and the Axis developed during the war. It also proved an important Cold War propaganda tool in showing that capitalism was capable of monumental planned development. Rational

---

5   Wilson, *America's Johannesburg*, 163.

planners imagined themselves to be efficient, scientific, apolitical experts, who could collect and evaluate all the relevant
data and interests for a given area, and use complex modeling,
land use controls and state police power to remake central cities.
This claim to objectivity, however, masked a strong ideology
that planners knew better than those whose spaces were being
planned, and that the interests of cities were closely aligned
with those of racial capitalism.

In its radical form, rational comprehensive planning could
also produce awesome feats of "militant modernism," including large-scale systems of public housing, education, health and
transit produced at the behest of powerful popular movements.[6]
During this period, many cities adopted rent control systems,
which used intricate formulas to determine how much rents
could rise annually and provided stability for tenants (and landlords too). Such public-spirited planning, however, was more the
exception than the rule. It was rational planners who oversaw
the redlining of central cities—in which bankers were given free
rein to deny loans in Black and immigrant neighborhoods—as
well as the sprawling expansion of White-only suburbs. And it
was rational planners who enacted so-called "urban renewal"
plans in cities across the country, which displaced hundreds of
thousands of people by demolishing long-standing working
class and industrial neighborhoods and replacing them with
highways and high-rise residential and office towers.

These plans met sustained resistance from local communities
whose neighborhoods had been written off as "blighted" and

---

6   Hatherley, Owen. *Militant modernism*. John Hunt Publishing, 2009.

obsolete. Caribbean Brooklynites formed mutual aid societies to combat the economic assault of redlining. Puerto Rican tenants on Manhattan's West Side refused to leave their buildings, even as bulldozers gathered to clear the way for Lincoln Center. Fighting alongside them were practitioners of a confrontational new mode of planning that emerged in direct response to rational comprehensive planning: *advocacy planning*. Advocacy planners rejected the idea that professionals could forge a rational consensus between opposing interests, or that planners should view the city from on high. Instead, they believed that neighborhoods should create their own community-based plans in direct opposition to the state. One of the most effective advocacy planners was Walter Thabit, a New York City planner who joined with residents of the Cooper Square section of Manhattan to stop the city from demolishing their neighborhood and help envision an alternative. After fifty years of struggle, Cooper Square now operates as a community land trust, and most of the housing will remain genuinely affordable in perpetuity.

Many advocacy planners took their critique directly into the state and joined city planning departments as *equity planners*. The most celebrated among them is Norman Krumholz, who spent decades fighting from inside Cleveland's planning bureaucracy, but equity planners also worked in Bernie Sanders' Burlington, Harold Washington's Chicago and more, helping to shift their cities planning priorities leftward while building institutional mechanisms for popular expressions of power. Advocacy and equity planners' critique of rational comprehensive planning was itself attacked from the left by scholars like Frances Fox Piven, who argued that they were diverting poor communities from more disruptive and effective forms of protest, but it nonetheless provided a platform for more confrontational forms of planning.[7]

Advocacy and equity planning, however, were not the only responses to rational comprehensive planning. From the right, the critique took the form of *incremental planning*. Incrementalists argued that the problem with rational planners was less their racism than their ambition. Big plans reeked of state-powered social engineering, and of an epistemological overconfidence in planners' abilities. Instead, they proposed that planners practice "the science of 'muddling through,'" or a trial-and-error approach that valued stability over transformation.[8] While more modest in its goals than its left counterparts (advocacy and equity planning), incrementalism had an enormous influence on the profession, which was suffering a crisis of confidence at exactly the moment when conservative political elements were seeking to dismantle its power.

In the early 1970s, the United States and much of the world underwent a number of critical economic and political realignments that are often described as the "neoliberal turn." The state's function turned from modest welfare toward gross deregulation; public policy marginalized the industrial sectors of the economy and elevated finance, insurance and real estate (FIRE); eventually, the role of city planners devolved

---

7   Piven, Frances Fox. "Whom does the advocate planner serve?" *Social Policy* 1.1 (1970): 32–35.

8   Lindblom, Charles E. "The science of 'muddling through.'" *Public Administration Review* 19.2 (1959): 79–88.

from reshaping space to retaining investment. In many cities, this transition began with neoliberalism's close cousin, neoconservatism. In New York, following the fiscal crisis of 1975, planners—informed by studies produced by the RAND Corporation—instituted a harsh program known as "planned shrinkage," in which city services (such as fire houses and public hospitals) were shuttered in order to encourage poor people of color to exit the city. Former Trotskyite-turned-neoconservative planning commissioner Roger Starr defended the policies as an attempt to "stop the Puerto Ricans and the rural Blacks from living in the city … Our urban system is based on the theory of taking the peasant and turning him into an industrial worker. Now there are no industrial jobs. Why not keep him a peasant?"[9]

Neoconservative planners starved their cities; *neoliberals* begged capitalists to feed off them. "Economic development" specialists became competitive sales representatives for their cities, citing low taxes and limited regulation as reasons for investors to choose their towns. By the 1990s, the line between planners and real estate developers blurred as "new urbanism"—a movement to make the suburbs great again—became the vague watchwords of builders and bureaucrats alike. Public-private partnerships flourished, as planners increasingly sought profit-oriented entities to do the work of urban design, construction and maintenance. *Communicative planning* became the primary professional mode, focusing less on changing cities (or, in one proponent's terms, "going beyond a preoccupation with the distribution of material

---

9   *Real Estate Weekly*, February 9, 1976; as quoted in Fitch, Robert. *The assassination of New York*. Verso, 1993, viii.

resources") than on listening to all the relevant "stakeholders" and crafting a balanced response.[10] While prior planning movements could be criticized as elitist and in service to capital, they nonetheless produced spaces for large elements of the public to use and enjoy. In the neoliberal era, the trend in planning became private development for private accumulation—damn the public.

Why Capitalist Cities Plan

Planners tend to be inordinately nice people. They gravitate to the profession out of a desire to help their cities and improve living conditions for their neighbors. Most planners do not seek to line the pockets of wealthy elites or displace the poor. And yet that is exactly what has happened, again and again, in city after city, across the United States and throughout the capitalist world. If the personal motivations of planners cannot explain this dynamic, how do we account for it? What is urban planning's role in the maintenance of capitalism, and all the exploitation and appropriation that system engenders?

The history of capitalism clearly shows that market economies require planning. Despite the protestations of libertarian absolutists, markets do not emerge from a state of nature, nor are they the product of simple evolution from prior economic modes. They are carefully planned, crafted and controlled. They rely on massive legal, logistical, infrastructural and technical capacities, all of which must not only be imagined and

---

10   Healey, Patsy. "The communicative turn in planning theory and its implications for spatial strategy formation." *Environment and Planning B: Planning and design* 23.2 (1996), 219.

developed but likewise maintained and reproduced. They require the coercive power of militaries and police, which themselves require massive amounts of planning to accomplish such plunder and enclosure. And eventually they come to demand their own regulation, both to establish a predictable ground on which to operate and to create a suitable barrier against upstart competition. To be sure, planning can also get in the way of markets, whether by imposing price controls or by defending public space. But if planners help the state establish spatial order over time, and if the state under capitalism is fundamentally "the executive committee of the bourgeoisie," then planners—whatever their intention—are working for the maintenance, defense and expansion of capitalism.[11]

Planners are also responsible for maintaining the spatial dimension of racial inequalities. Capitalism is always racial—though the precise meaning and articulation of racial differentiation and domination varies and changes over time and place. In all instances, however, capitalism produces powerful racial ideologies, a set of human categories with supposedly inborn and homogeneous traits that legitimate the system's inherent inequalities. Within the capitalist state, planners are tasked with reproducing this racist order through a series of supposedly race-neutral tools that are, in reality, anything but. The clearest examples are zoning and urban renewal, two policies whose formal raison d'être is to create rational and orderly urban landscapes; in reality, however, these tools are often used

---

11 Marx, Karl and Friedrich Engels. *The communist manifesto*. League for Industrial Democracy, 1933 [1848].

to target one racial group for exclusion or expulsion while clear-
ing the way for another's quality of life. Planning itself is not
inherently racist; in fact, it is central to racism's negation. But
racial capitalism asks planners to sort out who will go where,
under what conditions and for whose benefit.

Such actions are intrinsically coercive. Planners often
describe the force underlying their work as "police power."
This authority, however, is more commonly expressed through
compelled consent than through overt force. The built environment that planners establish is itself a means of securing
consent; you don't go where you're blocked from going,
whether by a road pattern, a fence or a wall. Planners also
secure consent by cloaking their power in rationality. While the
capitalist state can be considered a "dictatorship of the bourgeoisie," it often operates as a republic with some democratic
features.[12] For the most part, planners cannot simply foist their
plans onto the public, but must convince them that these plans
are in fact the most rational option. As planning theorist Bent
Flyvbjerg maintains, however, "power defines reality" and
"rationalization presented as rationality is a principal strategy
in the exercise of power."[13] One of the main tasks of urban
planning, then, is to make capitalist development appear to
be in the rational best interests of workers and bosses alike.

In order for capitalist development to work, though, planners need to look out for peoples' survival in a way that capital

---

12   James, Cyril Lionel Robert. *Modern politics*. PM Press, 2013 [1960],
47–48.
13   Flyvbjerg, Bent. *Rationality and power: Democracy in practice*. University
of Chicago Press, 1998, 227–28.

cannot—or will not—do. This recalls Fred Moten and Stefano Harney's definition of planning as "self-sufficiency at the social level."[14] The market alone will never fully meet the working class' daily needs: wages are too low for food, and have to be supplemented with welfare or direct provisions; transportation costs are borne by the individual worker, who needs mass transit to get around; housing is perpetually beyond the means of working and poor city dwellers, thus requiring the state to offer public, subsidized and regulated housing. While buildings and bridges are the iconic imagery of cities and planning, the hidden work of social reproduction—housing, health care, education, food, culture, comradery—is what truly allows capitalist cities to work, and is thus a central preoccupation of city planners.

Most of this work—production, consumption, social reproduction—takes place on land that is privately owned but publicly managed. Land is a particularly complicated factor in capitalism, as it is both a precondition for all commodities' production and circulation, and a strange sort of commodity in and of itself. Land is not traded like other products. Instead, according to geographer David Harvey, land "is a fictitious form of capital that derives from expectations of future rents."[15] These future rents are highly susceptible to external factors, such as pollution, zoning or the vagaries of demand.

About thirty years ago, planning scholar Richard Foglesong examined leftist theories of land in relation to urban planning

---

14 Moten, Fred and Stefano Harney. *The undercommons: Fugitive planning and Black study*. Minor Compositions, 2013, 76.
15 Harvey, David. *Rebel cities: From the right to the city to the urban revolution*. Verso Books, 2012, 28.

during the first 300 years of what would become the United States, and produced perhaps the most elegant explanation of planning's function in capitalist cities. He noticed that the central conflict in this history was between the "social character of land"—or its value as "a collective good, a social resource"—and its private ownership and control. From this conflict arose two contradictions—the *property contradiction* and the *capitalist-democracy contradiction*—and it fell on professional urban planners to handle them.[16]

The *property contradiction* describes the unhappy tension between capitalists' desire for certain types of planning interventions and their antipathy toward anything that restricts their operations. They need government to undertake certain functions to secure both their own profitability and their workers' survival; they demand that the state build the infrastructure that makes their land usable, such as roads, train tracks, water and sewer systems; and they demand that the state care for their employees through basic welfare functions, such as emergency health care and public education, in order to ensure a reliable source of labor.

Different types of capitalists, however, make different demands on the state. Industrial landholders reject environmentally strenuous zoning that restricts the location of their operations in the city; real estate capitalists would welcome such regulations because pollution diminishes their property values. Industrial capitalists might demand affordable housing for their workforce in order to stave off demands for raises;

---

16   Foglesong, Richard E. *Planning the capitalist city: The colonial era to the 1920s*. Princeton University Press, 1986.

real estate capitalists would object to any constraint on their ability to maximize rental or sale profits.

While capitalists need a lot from planners (even if they can't agree among themselves as to what, exactly, they want), they are also fiercely protective of their property rights. They know that private property laws are the only thing keeping their workers or tenants from expropriating them out of business, and therefore tend to be broadly suspicious of state interventions that could theoretically impinge on property rights. They know their land would be useless without planners, but they reject planning as such as an expression of government overreach. This, in short, is the property contradiction.

A second key phenomenon, the *capitalist-democracy contradiction*, is borne directly out of liberal governments' attempts to deal with the property contradiction. In a nominally democratic capitalist republic, the state and its planners have to perform a delicate balancing act: planners must proceed with enough openness and transparency to maintain public legitimacy, while ensuring that capital retains ultimate control over the processes' parameters. The people must have their say, but their options must be limited. If the system is entirely opened up, people might demand the full socialization of land, the abolition of private property and all the rest. If the system is completely closed, however, they might revolt against an unjust and unaccountable government. Planners are therefore tasked with creating public processes that are open but rigged. From this capitalist-democracy contradiction arises the familiar landscape of "participatory planning"—public comment periods, community boards, planning commissions, design charettes and a host of other interventions.

According to this model, urban planners' main job is to contain these two contradictions; neither can be resolved, but both can be managed. This puts city planners in a complicated bind. They are encouraged to make certain land use interventions, but are prevented from making more sweeping changes. Planners operate in a system that must appear open to the public, while simultaneously guaranteeing that ultimate power resides in the hands of propertied elites. It can be a really shitty job.

The Real Estate State

Three decades after Foglesong presented his contradictions, many of these conditions are still in place: planners still have to balance capitalists' demand for intervention and fear of domination; and planners still must uphold a precarious equilibrium between public participation and private control. But one key factor has changed. Throughout the 300-year period covered by Foglesong in *Planning the Capitalist City*, manufacturing capital was a serious player in municipal politics; and yet, by the book's publication in 1986, US industry had already undergone remarkable central-city contractions, with its urban political influence diminishing in turn. Today, in much of the country, manufacturing capital is not a leading force in urban politics. In most cities and towns, real estate rules.

Of course, other strands of capital make important claims on the city and its management. Finance continues to be a major force in New York City politics, but it is so thoroughly integrated with real estate—and has been for so long—that it is hardly an independent influence. Technology firms are at the heart of San Francisco's new political economy, but their vision of the city is all about private property and profitability and thus retains a central role for real estate. (In the case of Airbnb, big tech and real estate capital are one and the same.) Although Ford and General Motors still make some cars in Detroit and Dearborn, their presence there is also felt through corporate headquarters and downtown real estate holdings. Financial offshoots like Ford Credit and General Motors Financial are now among the most profitable aspects of the auto industry.

Even though manufacturing capital is less of a force in US urban politics than in the past, the industrial sector has certainly not disappeared. The world is more industrialized than ever, and the United States still produces plenty of goods. In fact, manufacturing remains the most important sector of the US economy in terms of total output. What has happened is a major geographical reorganization in production and distribution. Over the past seventy-five years, the United States has gone through three major industrial shifts: a movement of parts and assembly plants from older northern cities to newer southern cities and rural areas from roughly 1947 to 1973; a deeper set of national and international production relocations from 1973 through the 1980s and 1990s; and finally, in the 1990s and 2000s, an expansion of logistics clusters that coordinate the flow of goods into and out of population centers around the country.

As a result of these relocations, much of the United States' industrial activity today takes place outside the big cities: giant food processing plants in exurban areas; energy extraction centers on Appalachian mountaintops and Gulf coast outposts; and, most importantly for big cities, growing import/

export processing zones in major metropolitan areas. These distribution hubs employ enormous numbers of workers but, because of their demand for fast access out of central city traffic, their sprawling size, and the high cost and regulation of central city land, they tend to be located outside the political boundaries of the main cities they serve. Crucially, this means they make fewer land- and housing-based demands of city planners in places like New York, Los Angeles and Chicago than centrally located urban factory owners would. When these logistics clusters are located inside the political boundaries of major cities—like New York's Hunts Point Market and JFK Airport—they often operate on public land, meaning the companies that depend on them are not particularly bothered by the cost of urban land and housing (particularly if they assume their workers will live in cheaper suburbs or exurbs). In fact, since publicly operated logistics clusters are largely financed through municipal bonds, city governments may see inducing gentrification—something bond buyers generally interpret as a sign of urban health and future wealth—as key to financing this increasingly important form of urban industry.

The United States' most important urban industrial sector, then, does not act as a powerful counterweight to real estate in central city planning and development politics. Real estate does not itself constitute a new urban economy; its locational value is still dependent on proximity to other productive economic forces, usually in the expansive service sectors. Still, real estate's gargantuan growth manages to overdetermine cities' economic, political and demographic futures, pricing out certain actors and industries while encouraging others. In the absence of any major competition, real estate dominates contemporary urban planning.

This is not a uniquely American phenomenon; as the global 1 percent reaps the majority of the world's economic growth, they have formed what one analyst calls "a Niagara of capital into real estate" and shifted the bulk of their investments toward property over all other forms of economic activity.[17] Building booms are eating up cities around the world, from London to Mumbai to Nairobi to São Paulo and, of course, New York, where enormous, expensive and largely uninhabited investment properties float menacingly above scenes of homelessness and deprivation. Vancouver planner Andy Yan labels this the "hedge city" phenomenon, or the way the world's wealthiest are transforming urban high-rises from "machines for living in" to machines for money laundering.[18] Such cities have seen their housing prices balloon over 50 percent in the past five years; in some places, far more.[19]

This is an extremely precarious position. Each of New York's previous periods of massive skyscraper construction tracked with spectacular speculative booms and subsequent busts—1929, 1973, 1987, 2000 and 2008.[20] With every cycle, the number of high-rises climbed higher, monuments to the growing price of real estate that underwrote their elevation. After the crash of 2008, however, US property values only dropped momentarily

---

17 Downs, Anthony. *Niagara of capital: How global capital has transformed housing and real estate markets*. Urban Land Institute, 2007, 1.

18 Surowiecki, James. "Real estate goes global." *New Yorker*, May 26, 2014.

19 Leilani, "Report of the special rapporteur on adequate housing."

20 Harvey, *Rebel cities*, 32–34.

before restarting their steady uptick. Even as single-family homes around the country were foreclosed, they were often resold to private equity firms and rented for significant profit, contributing to a nationwide spike in evictions. With planners' help, real estate capital has been able to turn such crises into new opportunities.

The opportunity to benefit from property booms, however, is never universal. In the United States, real property has always been patterned by racism and sexism, its most brutal expressions being "manifest destiny" and slavery. While the real estate industry exploits people of all backgrounds, long-standing racial inequities have allowed White wealth to be passed down generationally through inherited housing and the profit from its sale. Where wider opportunities for ownership have arisen, the real estate industry has repeatedly tested its most exploitive innovations—from contract housing to subprime lending—on women and people of color, who were long shut out of standard credit markets. Imani Henry of Brooklyn's Equality for Flatbush sees in the current property boom "a whole new wave" of exploitive real estate practices. "In Flatbush, real estate agents have told me they aren't even allowed to rent to Black people anymore. Landlords want to flip everything here and kick us out to New Jersey."[21] Real estate's rise is not a tide that lifts all boats, but a force that feeds off long-standing structural inequalities.

It also presents serious and specific problems for planners. In a private land market, all planning interventions will impact

---

21   Joseph, George. "Developers are 'very, very excited to pioneer' new neighborhoods under de Blasio's affordable housing plan." *Gothamist*, March 22, 2016.

land and property values either positively or negatively. Where there is an inter-capitalist feud between manufacturers and developers, a number of possibilities arise. The presence of industry, for example, means there is a capitalist—not only a labor—demand for government-sponsored affordable housing and rent control. It also means there is a powerful constituency that values lower, not higher, land values, since industrialists tend to see land and buildings as costs rather than assets. With the decline of urban industry, as well as the real and aspirational rise of homeownership among working and middle class people, the demand for lower land values comes only from organized renters. While urban tenant movements have secured important victories, they face a constant struggle against difficult odds. Assessing this political landscape, many nonprofits, unions and community-based organizations have determined that the most likely way to secure gains is through political programs that align with factions of real estate capital, such as development schemes that pair the construction of luxury housing with a modicum of affordable units, or labor peace deals that secure union status for workers in upscale developments. In manufacturing's absence, real estate holds something approaching monopoly power to shape the narrative around urban planning and urban futures.

At the same time, essential public services in most municipalities are funded through property taxes. The fate of public education, public libraries and public transit are therefore directly linked to the value of property and its rate of taxation. Places with high property values are able to maintain palatial public places, while cities with low property values suffer the indignities of crumbling buildings and broken services. Cities are incentivized to drive out anything that is understood to reduce property values: types of buildings, businesses, land uses or even people. While this has long been the case for suburbs, where industry and commerce are expected to be subordinate to residential land uses and segregation has long been a defining characteristic, it is increasingly true of cities, where real estate is becoming the primary commodity, revenue stream and political priority.

Under these conditions, planners managing the *property contradiction* are being asked to intervene in only one way: to do everything in their power to make land more expensive, and to do nothing that would challenge its status as a commodity rather than a commons. Central business district transportation and park plans? Great. Industrial retention and universal rent control? Maybe not.

Planners managing the *capitalist-democracy contradiction* are facing planning commissions and review boards comprised almost entirely of people whose futures are tied to real estate. To take New York as an example, at the time of this writing the Planning Commission is made up of four members with backgrounds in commercial real estate promotion, two luxury developers, two development consultants, a realtor, a nonprofit developer, a corporate lawyer, a business improvement district president and the building engineer behind Trump Tower.

This is the real estate state, a government by developers, for developers. It is not monolithic; there are plenty of disputes within it. Builders' desires are not always the same as owners', as reflected in the presence of separate developer and landlord lobbies in New York. Nonprofit developers follow a somewhat different model than for-profit builders. And of course government is still accountable to voters, who are by and large either renters or mortgage holders and continue to organize collectively against real estate's rule. But the parameters for planning are painfully narrow: land is a commodity and so is everything atop it; property rights are sacred and should never be impinged; a healthy real estate market is the measure of a healthy city; growth is good—in fact, growth is god.

It is a horrible atmosphere for planners interested in social reproduction, let alone social transformation. Planners are allowed to do little that won't raise property values. Often they do so directly and intentionally, by initiating rezonings, targeting tax breaks or gutting protective regulations in order to stimulate development. Just as often, however, increased property values are the result of genuine, socially beneficial land improvements. Public improvements become private investment opportunities as those who own the land reap the benefits of beautiful urban design and improved infrastructure. Those who cannot afford the resulting rising rents (or, in the case of homeowners, rising property assessments) are expelled: priced out, foreclosed, evicted, made homeless, or, in the best case scenario, granted a one-time buyout that will not afford them a new home in the neighborhood, or even the city.

Preservationist Michael Henry Adams has chronicled this dynamic as it unfolds in Harlem, where he has fought to maintain the tremendous record of Black history and culture that is contained in both the neighborhood's architecture and the memories of its long-term residents. He recounts a conversation between young people in the neighborhood, who were coming to terms with the greening of their block. After speaking with the children about his activism, Adams recalls one telling the others, "'You see, I told you they didn't plant those trees for us.' It was painful to realize how even a kid could see in every new building, every historic renovation, every boutique clothing shop—indeed in every tree and every flower in every park improvement—not a life-enhancing benefit, but a harbinger of his own displacement."[22] In the real estate state, planners can create marvelous environments for rich people, but if they work to improve poor peoples' spaces they risk sparking gentrification and displacement. Rich communities can lobby for all sorts of planning improvements, but many poor neighborhoods fight planning interventions they would otherwise embrace out of a very real fear that any enhancement will trigger displacement.

The promise of planning—of creating more beautiful cities; of imposing order on capital's chaos; of undoing the exploitive relations between people and land, and between city and country—is virtually impossible to realize under these conditions. Instead, the forces of property present two options for cities: gentrification or disinvestment. Other modalities surely exist, but they are made to feel increasingly unlikely under real estate's rule, which pushes cities toward this binary. Urban planners' main task is ensuring that the former, rather than the latter, represents their city's lot.

---

22 Adams, Michael Henry. "The end of Black Harlem." *New York Times*, May 27, 2016.

2

Planning Gentrification

What is happening to our cities?
Why are they becoming so impossibly expensive?

Healthy cities exist in a state of flux. Change is necessary and good: people come and go, are born and die; industries are carefully harnessed, but almost never become permanent fixtures. A city that never changes is probably not a city at all.

But a particular kind of change is taking hold in many cities and towns around the world—one that presents itself as neighborhood revitalization but results in physical displacement and social disruption for the urban working class. In geographer Ipsita Chatterjee's terms, it represents "the theft of space from labor and its conversion into spaces of profit."[1] This change is generally known as gentrification, the process by which capital is reinvested in urban neighborhoods, and poorer residents and their cultural products are displaced and replaced by richer people and their preferred aesthetics and amenities.

---

1   Chatterjee, Ipsita. *Displacement, revolution, and new urban politics: Theories and case studies*. Sage, 2014, 5.

Every time it happens it looks somewhat different. Spatial transformations are always premised on local political-economic conditions and shaped by particular narratives and ideologies that are specific to each location. But there are some features that occur again and again.

Low rents become high. Landlords and speculators profit from the eviction of long-term tenants, who are forced to live farther and farther from their jobs and communities. As space-time contracts for wealthier people moving closer to their central city jobs, it expands for those pushed to the geographical limits of metropolitan areas. Bankers walk to work while debtors endure super-commutes.

The people of color and immigrants who built up neglected neighborhoods are recast as outsiders in their own homes and expelled in favor of White newcomers. Neighborhoods and, eventually, cities become places only the rich can afford, with environments designed according to their desires.

The commercial fabric turns over and replaces itself. Existing bars, restaurants, coffee shops, supermarkets, hardware stores and other everyday urban spots are deemed deficient, and are replaced by new bars, restaurants, coffee shops, supermarkets and hardware stores deemed superior largely because they charge higher prices and pay higher rents.

Municipal investment follows real estate investment. After years of complaints about failing schools and subpar parks, new funding suddenly manifests. Though residents used buses and bicycles before, new lanes dot the landscape once new money arrives. These benefits appear as long-term residents are priced out and have to find homes in other divested communities.

All this change does not just happen on its own. It requires investors, developers and landlords—the "producers" of gentrification—to buy and sell land and buildings at ever higher costs. It also requires wealthier homebuyers, renters and shoppers—the "consumers" of gentrification—to valorize areas they would have previously ignored. Neither side alone makes gentrification a reality, since economic value is only realized when both production and consumption demands are fulfilled. If producers build but consumers don't bite, the market busts; likewise, if consumers are prepared to purchase but producers don't invest, the result is unmet demand.

Part of what planners do, then, is ensure that both sides of the relationship are present by luring gentrification's producers with land use and tax incentives, while inviting its consumers through race- and class-inflected neighborhood initiatives. The state is a central actor, marshaling investment, boosting land values, attracting desired residents and industries, chasing away threats to profits and rolling out the welcome mat for developers and investors. Gentrification, then, is a political process as well as an economic and social one; it is planned by the state as much as it is produced by developers and consumed by the condo crowd. Planners did not invent gentrification, but they helped foster its development and transform it from a local phenomenon into a global business model.

Why Gentrification?

While land ownership, property development and speculative investment have always been part of the capitalist economy, until recently, real estate represented a smaller and more specialized business than industrial production. Like real estate, industry requires investments in land, infrastructure and buildings, but in an industrial context those features' worth tends to be a function of their productivity—if a factory were not productive, its buildings would not be considered valuable in and of themselves. Historically, as buildings aged their property values tended to drop, not climb, over time. The central city was the site of production and distribution, and those who lived closest to it usually could not afford to live farther away.

A number of changes in local, national and international political economies during the second half of the twentieth century, however, led investors away from industrial production in first-world cities. Global treaties among capitalist countries in the postwar era established organizations like the World Bank and the International Monetary Fund to facilitate low-cost global production and distribution of goods with minimal taxes and tariffs. Labor unions were attacked and marginalized, undermining their ability to act as a counter-hegemonic force for urban industrial retention. Advances in transportation technology and the standardization of containerized shipping made the exchange of goods across space a much simpler and cheaper proposition, and required a different spatial layout than most central city planners and politicians were willing or able to provide. Real estate-minded city planners actively pushed industry out with land use changes and redevelopment projects meant to marginalize manufacturing while driving up land costs.

As a result of these and other changes, during the second half of the twentieth century industry decamped from many first-world central cities in search of lower wages, looser environmental standards and wide-open spaces in northern suburbs, rural towns and international "free trade zones." New York City is an extreme but telling example: from the 1950s to the 1990s, the city lost 750,000 manufacturing jobs while its land values soared from $20 billion to $400 billion.[2]

As the complex process of deindustrialization unfolded, capital became both more mobile and, ironically, more grounded: tariffs dropped, firms internationalized and corporate globalization took hold while, at the same time, investments in land and buildings filled the literal and figurative space left by urban industrial flight. Real estate went from being a secondary to a primary source of urban capital accumulation. This switch is the genesis of gentrification in the United States.

US urban property investments were patterned by two prior federal programs, redlining and urban renewal. During the postwar era of rational comprehensive planning, the primary project of real estate capital was suburbanization. Massive amounts of public and private money poured in to create segregated residential enclaves located outside central cities and connected by new highways and railways. In the 1950s and '60s, city governments responded with "urban renewal" programs, in which entire working class and industrial neighborhoods were bulldozed to make way for central business district expansions and infrastructure projects. While

2 Fitch, *The assassination of New York*, 40.

some low-income developments were produced through these programs—including much of the country's public housing—90 percent of new residential construction was designed for middle- and upper-class households.[3] Robert Fitch called it "real estate Stalinism."[4] With markers of poverty cleared, more city space was produced and coded for urban real estate investment and development.

Even before bulldozers cleared the way for cranes, bankers and planners had set out on a stealthier form of urban neighborhood clearance, which established the preconditions for gentrification. In 1934 New Deal legislation established the Federal Housing Administration (FHA) to standardize, regulate and insure home mortgages. Not everyone, however, could access these loans. Along with the FHA, the federal government empowered bankers and developers to lead the Home Owners' Loan Corporation (HOLC). HOLC was tasked with quantifying the risk bankers would take in giving loans to particular people in particular places. This would allow the federal government and the banks to agree on rates for FHA loan insurance. To make these decisions, HOLC sent surveyors out to every residential block in just about every city in the country; those surveyors would look at a neighborhood and grade it on a scale from A (very safe) to D (very unsafe).

There were three main criteria HOLC used to determine risk: 1) the age of the building stock; 2) the density of housing; and, by far most determinately, 3) the racial composition

---

3   O'Connor, James. *The fiscal crisis of the state*. St. Martins Press, 1973, 147.

4   Fitch, *The assassination of New York*, 141.

of residents. Jews were considered communistic and likely to go on rent strike. Italians were characterized as dangerous gangsters. African Americans were written off entirely, and virtually any block with any Black people was given a low grade. Following real estate industry "best practices," the FHA made segregation and suburbanization the United States' de facto housing policy. Over time, as property owners in Black, immigrant and racially mixed neighborhoods were shut out of the finance system, many of their buildings declined, rents fell and some landlords resorted to abandonment.

One landlord's abandonment, however, is another buyer's opportunity, and in the 1960s, '70s and '80s many young urbanites, as well as a few farseeing financiers, saw an opportunity to grab low-cost properties and renovate them. "Brownstoning" and "loft living" became touchstones for young artists and professionals seeking urban "authenticity" and alternatives to the dominant pro-suburban narratives of the 1950s and 1960s. Although many considered themselves architectural preservationists, few paid much attention to preserving their neighborhood's social character. Many of these new brownstone owners evicted all of their tenants and converted their buildings into single-family homes, while loft landlords actively pushed out their remaining industrial tenants in favor of residential converters.

In several cities, these trends coincided with a severe round of fiscal crises and capital strikes—moments when a state cannot raise the capital it needs to maintain its budgets and bond investors refuse to buy shares in its future. New York's late-1970s recovery from the brink of bankruptcy was led by banks, real estate interests and municipal unions, who disciplined the city through a process of privatization and disinvestment from social services that continues to this day. Municipal wages and benefits were slashed; welfare payments fell by one-third; the city's public universities started charging tuitions. Meanwhile, stock taxes were dropped, income taxes were halved and real estate taxes fell to historic levels. This became a model for neoliberal governments throughout the country and around the world.

During this process, gentrification presented an alternative way for cities to continue redeveloping their housing stock and boosting land values without (at first) spending much money. Over time the model proved effective, and local governments, banks and major real estate firms got into the business of financing gentrification, either through loans to high-income homeowners in places that were previously redlined, or by building luxury landscapes in neighborhoods that had long been considered unsafe for investment.

Gentrification, then, was a "spatial fix" for capitalism's urban crisis: a way to profit from previous disasters and to find new places for investors to turn money into more money.[5] Deindustrialization created the space for real estate's revival, and redlining and urban renewal set the spatial patterns for disinvestment and reinvestment. What first appeared as an opportunistic venture for middle class movers and profit-seeking landlords—a building-by-building, block-by-block phenomenon—became a way to transform entire cities from places into products.

---

5   Harvey, David. *The limits to capital*. Verso, 1982.

The Economics of Gentrification

By definition, gentrification cannot happen everywhere. It is the third stage in a long-term process of capital flow in and out of space: first comes *investment* in a built environment; second, neighborhood *disinvestment* and property abandonment; and third, *reinvestment* in that same space for greater profits. The key to understanding why some places gentrify is the amount of money that a landowner—who effectively holds a monopoly on all rents from a particular geographic location—can expect to generate from a given lot and the building atop it. Real estate speculators choose to invest in a particular location because they identify a gap between the rents that land currently offers and the potential future rents it might command if some action were taken, such as evicting long-term tenants, renovating neglected or unstylish properties, or demolishing and reconstructing buildings.

Geographer Neil Smith proposed this thesis in 1979 as the primary driver of gentrification at the building level. Gentrification, he theorized, "occurs when the gap is wide enough that developers can purchase shells cheaply, can pay the builders' costs and profit for rehabilitation, can pay interest on mortgage and construction loans, and can then sell the end product for a sale price that leaves a satisfactory return to the developer."[6] Smith formulated this theory during a period of urban disinvestment, when the *rent gap* described the space between falling actual rents and stable or slowly rising potential rents.

---

6   Smith, Neil. "Toward a theory of gentrification: A back to the city movement by capital, not people." *Journal of the American Planning Association* 45.4 (1979): 538–48, 545.

In today's context, the rent gap in hyper-invested cities like New York is more likely to be between slowly rising actual rents and exploding potential rents.

Under these conditions, rent gaps exist at more than just the building scale. When enough individual buildings in an area are brought up to their full potential rents, the remaining surrounding properties exhibit a rent gap (as does the entire neighborhood). The rent regulations that govern prices and tenure rights for nearly half the private rental apartments in New York have tenuously kept hundreds of thousands of apartments at below-market rents. This creates a citywide rent gap that landlords are working hard to close through evictions and demolitions as well as political lobbying.

In some markets, real estate firms try to profit from the potential value of their properties by selling rather than renting them. This can take the form of townhouses being converted from apartment buildings to single-family homes, or individual apartments in larger buildings being sold as co-ops or condominiums. As the market for such housing rises in cities around the world, the *value gap* between the income they generate as rental properties and their potential sale price expands and the potential for gentrification rises.

A similar dynamic exists in places where a property's current use masks the potential income that property could generate if it were given over to another activity. The clearest example of this *functional gap* would be the remaining factories in central city locations. In Manhattan's Chinatown, for example, the garment industry—which by the 1980s employed roughly 20,000 people in 500 shops—has now nearly vanished, not only because of

competition from cheap imports but also because of a widening
functional gap: the difference between current manufacturing
rents and potential residential or commercial rents became so
great that building owners were willing to evict their industrial
tenants to make room for higher paying alternatives. By now,
most of Chinatown's factories have been converted into offices,
hotels or condominiums, forcing the workforce that sustained
them to shift to service-sector jobs, while enabling the industrialists who ran them to move on to other, more profitable
pursuits. John Lam, one of the neighborhood's most infamous
garment titans, went from owning fifteen factories, employing
1,200 workers and doing over $40 million in business annually to
being one of the "undisputed titans of Manhattan's hotel scene."[7]

By the twenty-first century, real estate developers and city
planners learned how to identify and exploit these opportunities, turning grit into gold. They developed housing, policing,
education and design strategies to identify rent, value and
functional gaps, and encouraged speculators to close them.

This has given rise to new and peculiar forms of gentrification.
Rich neighborhoods that never truly experienced disinvestment
have become "super-gentrified," with homes in places like
New York's Greenwich Village and Brooklyn Heights selling for astronomical figures to finance titans, and unregulated
rents pricing out even relatively wealthy households.[8] Far

---

7   Kwong, Peter. *The new Chinatown*. Hill and Wang, 1987; Schram, Lauren
Elkies. "Ex-Partners Sam Chang and John Lam Are the Undisputed Titans of
Manhattan's Hotel Scene." *Commercial Observer*, October 8, 2015.

8   Lees, Loretta. "Super-gentrification: The case of Brooklyn Heights,
New York City." *Urban Studies* 40.12 (2003): 2487–2509.

from central cities, some rural towns are moving through the phases of gentrification, with rent gaps making historic barn houses and ranch-side cottages alluring sites for speculative investment. Some rural areas, like billionaire Ted Turner's sprawling 2 million-acre ranches in Montana and New Mexico, are gentrified virtually overnight and send their effects rippling outward through the local land market. Meanwhile, billionaires like Warren Buffett and Sam Zell are buying up trailer parks and raising rents for tenants, many of whom are displaced urbanites. Beyond housing, global media corporations like Disney, Universal and Sony have worked with city planners to transform commercial areas such New Orleans' French Quarter and Manhattan's Times Square into gentrified tourist traps.

As much as the process mutates, it always retains its core: landlords and developers identify gaps and act to close them. In most cases, however, it's not just capitalists initiating the process, but also local state actors who, in responding to the changing economic landscape as well as the demands of specific landholders, aim to lure investors and developers to particular areas. The politics of gentrification are therefore just as important as the economics.

The Politics of Gentrification

The emergence of gentrification in the late 1960s and '70s tracked closely with important political changes at the national and local levels. For gentrification's advance, the most significant was a shift in US cities' governing coalitions.

When manufacturing firms exited post-war urban centers, they left behind not just a tremendous amount of property but also a political vacuum. Since the industrial revolution took hold, cities had been governed by the political party that could best bridge the divide between the needs of industrial capital and its workforce. But with the flight of manufacturing from cities, real estate and finance became the remaining major urban power bloc and the key to rebuilding local economies.Real estate was an especially potent force in urban politics, because while finance can be ephemeral, real estate is always place-based.

This economic restructuring forced local governments to seek out new coalitions for securing political power. Being a friend of industry and a champion of industrial unions was no longer a viable strategy for winning (or financing) elections. By the late 1960s, it was becoming much more important to be a friend of real estate capital and the service and building trades unions.

This new growth coalition looked little like the old, and as a result some of the elected officials who rose to prominence during this transitional period—like New York's mayor, John Lindsay—were branded as refreshing reformers. They made common cause with the nascent community development movement, which, with support from federal anti-poverty programs and the Ford Foundation, was encouraging reinvestment in central city neighborhoods that had long been redlined or targeted for "urban renewal" clearance. They tweaked city land use laws to allow for a balance of renewed commercial development and historic preservation. They recognized that the country was moving toward social liberalism, and spurned overt racism and bigotry (without fully addressing the structural racism embedded in their policies and programs). They embraced art and cultural production as ways to bring people with money to their cities; when artists began renovating industrial lofts and middle class professionals were renovating brownstones, they saw a smart strategy for redevelopment that was simultaneously edgy and posh.

New regional blocs in New York City, along with Philadelphia, Pittsburgh, Baltimore, Washington, DC, and a number of other deindustrializing cities with historic housing stocks, made it part of their mission not only to encourage downtown construction, but to create policies that would hasten gentrification. The City Planning Commission's 1969 Plan for New York City stated, "If brownstoners have done what they have done in the face of major difficulties, it is staggering to think of what could be done if the difficulties were removed."[9] The plan proposed guaranteed mortgage loans for one- and two-family home purchases, long-term loans for renovations and tax abatements for home improvements.

Loft conversions were legalized and encouraged in sections of the city where planners wanted to spark industrial flight and residential reuse. Some housing leaders were initially bemused by the fury over "obsolete" loft buildings. Union co-op developer Abraham Kazan joked sardonically that "a finer collection of fire traps would be hard to find anywhere."[10] Over time,

---

9   "Plan for New York City 1969," as quoted in Whyte, William H. *City: Rediscovering the center*. Doubleday, 1988, 327–28.

10   Freeman, Joshua. *Working class New York: Life and labor since World War II*. New Press, 2000, 188.

however, many policymakers came to embrace the idea and were relieved to be dealing with artists demanding live-work spaces rather than impoverished tenants demanding livable conditions. In her book *Loft Living*, sociologist Sharon Zukin quotes a SoHo resident recalling a crucial public hearing on a proposed artists' district:

> [T]here were lots of other groups giving testimony on other matters. Poor people from the South Bronx and Bed-Stuy complaining about rats, rent control, and things like that. The board just shelved those matters and moved right along. They didn't know how to proceed. Then they came to us. All the press secretaries were there, and the journalists. The klieg lights went on, and the cameras started to roll. And all these guys started making speeches about the importance of art to New York City.[11]

Early gentrification was a boon to politicians who were both hamstrung by shrinking municipal budgets and unwilling to take on serious problems of entrenched poverty and structural racism. To their relief, the face of early gentrification was a group of middle class, mostly White liberals looking to add value to the city's building stock—just the kind of constituents they were seeking to cultivate. In many cities, these newcomers took over neighborhood associations, asserted their power within party clubs, and steered the work of local governance and planning bodies that had recently been created in response

11   Zukin, *Loft living*, 117–18.

to the urban civil rights struggles of the 1960s. In so doing, they exerted power far disproportionate to their actual numbers.

By the 1970s, conditions were in place to promote gentrification as a spatial fix for capital and a political fix for cities in crisis. It would take planners, however, to scale up gentrification from a neighborhood phenomenon of renovation and reinvention to a larger process of displacement, demolition and development.

Planners for Gentrification

Real estate fortunes are cyclical. The job of planners, then, is to keep business booming as long as possible, and when land and property values ultimately fall, to get them back up as quickly as possible. In order to do so, planners and policy elites have developed a wide range of mechanisms, which they put to use in various forms depending on particular local circumstances.

Local property tax cuts are one of the main incentives cities use to lure and retain real estate investment. They come in two main forms: those for renovation, and those for construction. In 1955, New York lawmakers created the J-51 tax abatement, which gives landlords a fourteen-year tax break for repairing their properties. In 1975 they expanded it to encourage industrial-to-residential conversions. At a cost of over $250 million per year in lost revenue, building owners continue to use J-51 to gut and renovate old buildings and drive up rents, or convert their rental properties into condominiums. In 1971, to spur new apartment construction, the city created the 421-a tax incentive program, which gives enormous tax breaks to luxury developers in gentrifying areas. By 2016, the program was costing the city $1.2 billion per year in lost property tax revenue; it was subsequently tweaked to extend the tax break at an estimated cost of $2.4 billion per year.[12]

Critics call this "geobribery"—the way planners use public finances to lure private investment into specific areas.[13] Among the most direct examples of geobribes are *Payment In Lieu of Taxes* (PILOT) projects, which have become commonplace in municipalities large and small. Under these schemes, developers pay a low annual fee to the municipality rather than a full tax load. Sometimes these deals are negotiated for deep-pocketed nonprofits or developers building on publicly owned (and therefore tax-exempt) land, but many cities—like New Jersey's Jersey City—have found ways to apply them more generally in order to incentivize downtown development. In some cases, in order to pay PILOTs instead of ordinary tax bills, for-profit developers will pay nonprofits to buy a piece of land, then lease it back to them. Cities get a little bit of cash from these deals, but they are often legally bound to use those funds to upgrade nearby infrastructure. In this sense, the developers win twice—they pay lower fees over time and they get improved public services.

An even grander geobribe is *Tax Increment Financing* (TIF), a widely used development incentive. Under TIF, planners usually start by designating an area as "blighted"—terminology

12   Waters, Tom. "Governor Cuomo's flawed 421-A proposal." *New York Slant*, November 29, 2016.
13   Roy, Ananya. "Why India cannot plan its cities: Informality, insurgence and the idiom of urbanization." *Planning Theory* 8.1 (2009): 76–87.

borrowed directly from "urban renewal" planning. Next, the city issues bonds for new infrastructure development in the district. After making improvements to the land and raising its value tremendously, the city hands the land to a developer, who builds private commercial or residential buildings. If their property values rise, their tax revenues are "captured" and used first to pay off bondholders, and then for renewed investment inside the TIF zone; if property values are stagnant or fall, the city is on the hook to pay back the bondholders. Risk is thus transferred from the private sector (real estate developers) to the public sector (the rest of us). When they fail, TIFs blow up budgets; when they are successful, they magnify uneven development. In such "successes," TIFs can generate more revenue than an entire city's municipal budget, reinforcing the disparity between gentrified and disinvested neighborhoods.

In addition to geobribery, planners have taken steps to surrender public ownership of land and buildings. One important manifestation is selling off tax-foreclosed properties acquired during recessions. In the wake of its mid-1970s fiscal crisis, New York City seized thousands of buildings when their owners stopped paying property taxes. In severely disinvested neighborhoods, this represented an enormous transfer of property and wealth; a 1983 study showed that 19,588 buildings had been taken in Harlem, representing more than a third of the total housing stock and nearly as many buildings as were owned by private landlords.[14] Some of these foreclosed buildings were

---

14   Schaffer, Richard and Neil Smith. The gentrification of Harlem? *Annals of the Association of American Geographers* 76.3 (1986): 347–65.

turned into limited-equity co-ops and controlled by former squatters. Most of them, however, were sold cheaply or given away to landlords who wanted to upgrade them. Years later, Obama's Housing and Urban Development secretary, Shaun Donovan, would look back on these actions as "the largest privatization of housing anywhere in the country."[15] This form of strategic liquidation played a large part in the gentrification of disinvested neighborhoods.

While cities were giving away their seized properties, many were also demolishing much—if not all—of their public housing. In conjunction with federal and state governments, cities across the country—from Atlanta to Chicago to Baltimore to New Orleans—severely underfunded their public housing and allowed projects to fall into dangerous disrepair. Building off architectural analyses and social science fads, many planners claimed the problem was bad design and a *concentration of poverty*—a problem they never seemed to associate with a concentration of wealth elsewhere. Financed by the federal government's HOPE VI program, these cities developed plans to destroy their public housing complexes and build small-scale, mixed-income, subsidized private housing wherever lots were available. The numbers of new apartments rarely came close to the number of homes destroyed, and they often cost significantly more to rent, but the process freed up coveted central city land for new development and gentrification.

---

15   Hevesi, Dennis. "Transforming city's housing: Act 2." *New York Times*, May 2, 2004.

As cities destroyed their public housing, they chipped away at rent controls or abandoned them altogether. This helped cement the relationship between planning and gentrification. With strong rent controls in place, urban planning interventions like new parks, schools and transit do not necessarily produce elevated housing costs; while public investments in neighborhoods might widen rent gaps, rent controls would prevent landlords from closing them. With rent controls diminished or removed, however, landlords could more easily raise rents based on new neighborhood improvements; they market these planning interventions as amenities for their property, and thus immediately turn inclusionary public investments into exclusionary private gains. Today a weak form of rent control still stands in some California, DC, Maryland, New York and New Jersey cities, but these systems have been systematically undermined by landlord-backed legislators and under-enforced by regulators. Many US states have passed ordinances outlawing further controls.

In addition to straightforward land giveaways and deregulation, planners have overseen a subtler but more systematic privatization of urban spaces. Historic gathering places have been turned over to private developers for the creation of *festival markets*—an economic development strategy that rarely benefits city residents as much as it does tourists and developers. Such projects, like Harborplace in Baltimore and South Street Seaport in New York, were especially popular among neoliberal planners in the 1970s and 1980s. Management of many older parks has been handed over to *conservancies*, who raise private funds for improvements and impose new rules that often target the poor. Newly designed public spaces are often privatized from the start. Not only do they come with conservancies attached to them, they are even sometimes private property—as in the case of New York City's privately owned public spaces. In cities throughout the country, commercial main streets are encouraged to form business improvement districts (BIDs), self-taxing entities run by and for landlords that collude to raise rents, bring in big box stores, and impose new security regimes on streets, sidewalks and public parks. Reflecting on the impact of one such BID on a strip of immigrant-owned small businesses, Tania Mattos of the group Queens Neighborhoods United recalled, "it used to be Calle Colombia. Now it's Calle Corporate."[16]

Likewise, planners have increasingly used zoning to facilitate gentrification. Zoning holds an outsized place in US municipal politics because of the particular dynamics of political devolution during the neoliberal period: responsibilities have been pushed to the local level, while control over policies and purse strings is held at higher governmental scales. For planners, this is a catch-22: cities are responsible for solving their own housing crises but the federal government restricts their abilities to build public housing and states often preclude them from enacting rent controls. Incentivizing development through zoning, then, becomes key to many municipal housing plans.

Both *upzoning* (which increases building density and development capacity) and *downzoning* (which limits it) can be used

---

16   Elstein, Aaron. "Shaping a neighborhood's destiny from the shadows." *Crain's New York Business*, September 18, 2016.

to channel investment to particular areas, and either open up new rent gaps or close them where they remain. More than almost any other tool in the planners' kit, zoning has tremendous impact on both land and property values. When a city upzones a particular lot, it makes that land far more valuable by increasing the amount of rent-producing units a developer can build. Upzoning can therefore encourage developers to buy existing properties, knock down the buildings and build something bigger. When planners downzone, they can dramatically raise property values for existing buildings, which may be bigger than the zoning allows for future developments. Downzoning can therefore encourage developers to reinvest in older properties and derive higher rents from existing buildings. In either case, planners produce enormous value with the stroke of a pen, and hand it over to land and property owners.

Rezoning can thus facilitate a vertical enclosure movement, which privatizes the air above and the ground below. In the case of upzonings, planners allow developers to own a new piece of the sky, turning everyone's airspace into someone's property. In the case of downzonings, planners can drive such schemes underground. In parts of central London, for example, where strict zoning caps limit building heights, property owners are allowed to create enormous and luxurious basements that elongate the boundaries of private property deep below the pavement.

Rezoning does not equal gentrification; under the right circumstances, zoning can be used to slow or even prevent gentrification. It can also be used to undo exclusionary land uses, like the giant single-family home zones that keep working class people out of sprawling, segregated suburbs. What zoning does is change the economic calculus of present versus future land uses. In conditions prone to gentrification—hyper-invested cities run by the real estate state—any rezoning will likely alter conditions such that landlord or developer incomes rise, and public benefits shrink.

Under these circumstances, even planners' provision of public goods—such as investments in schools, parks, transit and technology—tends to contribute to gentrification. The relationship, however, is complex.

Sometimes planners channel new services toward neighborhoods that are *already gentrified*, giving the wealthy the most resources even though their taxes go into a common municipal fund. This is the case, for example, when wealthy neighborhoods get better trash pickup than poorer ones, even though they are all served by the same sanitation department.

Sometimes planners invest in *currently gentrifying* areas in order to speed along the process. For example, when planners fix up the streets as rents start to rise, they are signaling to potential investors that these neighborhoods will no longer be neglected by the city.

And sometimes they focus their attention on areas that are *not yet undergoing gentrification* in order to attract real estate capital. This is the case when working class strongholds in gentrified cities are suddenly lavished with public attention—as in New York Governor Cuomo's plans for Brownsville, Brooklyn discussed in the Introduction. In all three cases, planners end up stimulating and compounding uneven development. This lose-lose-lose situation is one of the main reasons so many residents caught in the violence of gentrification are deeply skeptical of urban planners.

This violence is real and material: despite legal protections for tenants, landlords and their hired hands regularly seek to close rent gaps by force, using harassment, intimidation, eviction, and sometimes even arson, assault and murder. But it is not only owners who inflict this pain. Just as gentrification's violence is no metaphor, neither is planners' "police power."

Urban police forces act as the armed wing of the real estate state: what planners and policy makers enact, police enforce. Planning and police departments are separate entities, with separate leadership, budgets and institutional cultures. Their missions are nevertheless often aligned around protecting property and encouraging gentrification. Rising real estate values are a crucial performance metric for many urban police departments, who point to gentrification as proof that their ballooning budgets represent money well spent. With increased resources, police are mirroring planners by speaking the language of data-informed decision-making and adopting the tools of geographic information systems to target their activities. Using *quality of life* and *broken windows* campaigns, police aggressively stop, ticket, arrest, beat and even kill people accused of low-level infractions like loitering, unpermitted vending and turnstile jumping, particularly in gentrifying neighborhoods. This geographical targeting is neither incidental nor accidental: aggressive policing clears the terrain for future investment and makes wealthier households more comfortable with the idea of living among poorer people.

Planners do not encourage gentrification out of some undying commitment to violence, displacement or inequality; rather, gentrification is what happens when real estate rules and planners follow. Even if planners understand their work as promoting livability, growth and sustainability rather than as enabling inequality, as geographer Loretta Lees argues, "we need to see gentrification as mutating, as parasitic, as attaching to and living off other policies."[17] Whatever else they are working toward, planners in the real estate state are also planners for gentrification.

Justifying Gentrification

Mainstream planners recognize that gentrification presents both moral and economic problems for their cities. In rhetoric, they attest to the importance of balanced growth, inclusion and increased opportunity; in practice, however, most planners facilitate uneven development and measure their progress against rising land values. To bridge that gap, planners need theories and ideologies that let them feel altruistic while undermining the urban working class.

One of the most important is *highest and best use*. This concept turns land use planning into real estate appraisal, positing that the best use for any piece of land is that which derives the greatest value at the lowest cost and allows buildings to actualize their full potential rent. Measuring this, however, is nearly

---

17   Lees, Loretta. "The geography of gentrification: Thinking through comparative urbanism." *Progress in Human Geography* 36.2 (2012): 155–71, 163.

impossible, and always contested. Parks, for example, do not necessarily bring in much money, but they result in increased property values for the surrounding areas, which in turn deliver higher property tax revenues. The benefit of the park, then, is measured not just by its use and enjoyment, but by its value as a real estate amenity. Low-cost housing in the central city will rarely be a "higher" use than luxury housing, even if it is what most people in the city need. According to the theory, however, if planning is done according to highest and best use, then more money will land in the city's coffers and can be used for the social good. In the end, however, the copious real estate tax breaks that accompany this sort of planning ultimately rob the city of the very revenue that development is supposed to generate, creating little opportunity for income redistribution.

Often planners openly admit that they are trying to lift land values, but justify this action with attempts at *value recapture*—using tools that reclaim some social benefit from publicly generated private profits. Whenever cities upzone an area, for example, they create a rent gap out of thin air. In exchange, planners sometimes create mechanisms to "recapture" a portion of this value by demanding a public benefit from the landlord: an accessible open space in exchange for more development capacity (in the case of "privately owned public spaces"); a set of affordable apartments in new and bigger developments (in the case of "inclusionary zoning"); payment into a fund for nearby infrastructure improvements (in the case of PILOTs and TIFs); or a dedicated funding stream for transit that boosts property values (as in the case of New York City's proposed streetcar).

These policies are often considered progressive, since they make explicit demands on landlords and force them to pay their "fair share." This framing, however, has three major flaws. First, it assumes that planners must always give away value if they ever hope to win anything for the public. Actions that do not make money for landlords are therefore deemed worthless because they do not create any value to recapture. Second, it engages a sort of magical thinking whereby it is the landlords who actually pay these costs. Landlords' incomes come from tenants, so in the absence of very strong rent controls, the cost of these fees are more likely to be borne by renters than they are to cut into landlord profits. Third, it fails to account for the effects of increased property values in a private land market— i.e., gentrification. Even if some public benefits are secured at the site of the deal, residents who hope to enjoy them are at risk of displacement. As Marina Ortiz of the anti-gentrification group East Harlem Preservation admonishes, planners frame these value capture projects as "'looking toward the future,'— and that future will not include us."[18]

Whereas value recapture tends to add new regulations to the urban environment, other programs seek to remove regulations from working class districts. In these cases, planners seek to unlock what economist Michael Porter calls the *competitive advantage of the inner city*.[19] Porter argues that working class neighborhoods are underexploited markets that represent major

18 Savitch-Lew, Abigail. "4 months after rezoning, East Harlem stakeholders remain vigilant." *City Limits*, March 19, 2018.
19 Porter, Michael E. "The competitive advantage of the inner city." *Harvard Business Review* 73.3 (1995): 55–71.

opportunities for national retailers, and prescribes planning policies that clear the way for big box stores and large chain operations: lax zoning codes, loosened labor and environmental laws, and lower corporate taxes. The Clinton administration used this logic to promote "empowerment zones," a planning model derived from Margaret Thatcher's "enterprise zones" and recently rebranded and expanded by the Trump administration as "opportunity zones." In the name of increasing competitive advantage, these programs slash taxes and induce investment in areas that have not yet gentrified. In Harlem, the Clinton-era Empowerment Zone provided subsidies and protections to a host of incoming big box stores. Most of the decades-old Black-owned small businesses were pushed out of Harlem's main street, 125th, and several storefronts were replaced with a Harlem-themed shopping mall.

Another way planners carve out a competitive advantage is by luring the so-called *creative class*. This is a slippery social category that can mean anything from artists to tech workers and tends to focus more on high-end consumption habits than actual creative output. The language comes from planning theorist and consultant Richard Florida, who argues that cities today compete for their ability to attract and retain artists and idea creators.[20] Appeals to creativity do not automatically constitute gentrification; Floridian language aside, creativity is not actually a class trait and working class neighborhoods are always home to working class artists. What most planners take away from the concept, however, is that yuppies

---

20   Florida, Richard. *Cities and the creative class*. Routledge, 2005.

like artists, so cities should promote arts-based gentrification as a means to attract both. Planners then use lifestyle amenities and place-making strategies to attract capital—creative, as well as the more common kind. According to visual artist and Take Back the Bronx member Shellyne Rodriguez, "artists have this lingering stench that follows us around… It's a trojan horse tactic. You place art events in the middle of the community and then this shit starts to happen."[21]

Wrapped up in this "creative class" discourse is the notion of *livability*, or the idea that cities should be human scaled, environmentally sustainable and just plain nice. "Livability" can mean many things and can be a way to frame planning issues around the needs of people over profit. Most of the time, however, planners use "livability" to describe every urban nicety except the two most closely aligned with people's ability to live—the prices of labor and shelter. Like many planners, Amanda Burden, director of the New York City Planning Department under former mayor Bloomberg, used the word "livable" as a substitute for "gentrified." Referring to a neighborhood undergoing severe gentrification, Burden told the *New York Times*, "We are making so many more areas of the city livable. Now, young people are moving to neighborhoods like Crown Heights that 10 years ago wouldn't have been part of the lexicon."[22] No "livability" improvements are actually

---

21   Maleszka, Jamie. "Did Swizz Beatz's 'No Commission' art fair benefit the Bronx?" *Mass Appeal*, August 17, 2016.

22   Satow, Julie. "Amanda Burden wants to remake New York. She has 19 months left." *New York Times*, May 18, 2012.

specified, other than the presence of "young people," a euphemism for White people with disposable income.

One of the names most commonly associated with urban
livability is Jane Jacobs, a paradoxical hero of both leftist
advocacy planners and libertarian market urbanists. In her
1961 book *The Death and Life of Great American Cities*, as well
as in her later work, Jacobs pilloried the planning profession for creating sterile environments based on flawed ideas
about how people should interact with their surroundings.
As a writer as well as an organizer, she lashed out against
highway projects and modernist developments, and advo-
cated instead for the slow, organic growth of cities, centered
around vital and lively neighborhoods, short blocks, medium-
to-high densities, mixed uses, and a combination of new and
old buildings. She shook up the thinking around cities and
neighborhoods, and brought a feminist, street-level perspective to urban analysis.

The main lesson many planners pull from Jane Jacobs, however, is that gentrification is the best way to make cities more
livable. Planners around the country cite Jacobs when they
are tearing down housing projects or encouraging industrial
conversions. Airbnb, a firm targeted by tenant movements
for contributing to housing crises in cities around the world,
has sponsored "Jane's Walk NYC," a set of walking tours in
Jacobs' honor.

Jacobs, for her part, did not want to be associated with gentrification planning. In a note buried in her final book, she wrote
that the fight against gentrification was "unwinding vicious
spirals" that had resulted from well-intentioned projects:

By the end of the 1990s, gentrification was under way in what had been even the most dilapidated and abused districts of Manhattan. Again, the poor, evicted or priced out by the higher costs of renovating, were victims. Affordable housing could have been added as infill in parking lots and empty lots if government had been on its toes, and if communities had been self-confident and vigorous in making demands, but they almost never were. Gentrification benefited neighborhoods, but so much less than it could have if the displaced people had been recognized as community assets worth retaining. Sometimes when they were gone their loss was mourned by gentrifiers who complained that the community into which they had bought had become less lively and interesting.[23]

This analysis is at once prescient and deficient. It presents an alternative vision of economic development in which social preservation is as coveted as landmark preservation and livability is actually measured by people's ability to live in a place. But Jacobs unfairly faults communities for not fighting back and thus ignores the myriad examples of forceful activism that were contemporaneous to her argument. At the same time, she locates the problem in a government that was not "on its toes"; the issue was not that the state was unprepared for the developers sneaking into neighborhoods, but rather that it was functioning at a high capacity to invite them there. When Jacobs claims that "gentrification

---

23   Jacobs, Jane. *Dark age ahead*. Vintage, 2004, 214.

benefited neighborhoods," she presumably means that they became more livable for those who could afford to live there, and the physical qualities of the neighborhood—its buildings, shops and schoolhouses—were reinvested and upgraded. True as this might be, it elides the central lesson of Jacobs' work: that cities *are* their neighborhoods, and neighborhoods *are* their residents. To say that gentrification benefited neighborhoods while displacing its people flies in the face of this notion. When she writes that gentrification benefited neighborhoods "much less than it could have," she implies that the alternative should have been a friendlier form of gentrification, rather than another mode of urbanization altogether.

While Jacobs dreamed of a more livable gentrification, others argued that the standard mode was already livable enough. In the first decade of the twenty-first century, several prominent researchers produced studies claiming that gentrification was, on the whole, a positive force for cities and their residents. Geographer Tom Slater compiled an infuriating list of such studies and their media coverage, including New Urbanist planner Andres Duany's triumphalist "Three cheers of gentrification: It helps revive cities and doesn't hurt the poor" and Jacob Vigdor's 2002 Brookings Institute paper entitled "Does gentrification harm the poor?" (Answer: not particularly). Another report by economists Mckinnish, Walsh and White called "Who gentrifies low-income neighborhoods?" claimed that, in general, "it looks like gentrification is a pretty good thing." That report was picked up by *Time* magazine, who titled their article on the findings, "Gentrification: Not ousting the poor?"[24]

Using a version of the *neighborhood effects thesis*, or the idea that social outcomes are highly influenced by environmental factors, planning scholar Lance Freeman has presented research arguing that gentrification, while potentially disruptive, is not that bad for poor people.[25] Moreover, Freeman argues, gentrification does not actually cause much displacement; poor people move more than anyone else, he argues, but they are actually less likely to leave gentrifying neighborhoods because they enjoy the benefits that reinvestment brings. Many scholars disagreed with this analysis, as did many of those most vulnerable to gentrification, but it nonetheless fascinated planners and the press. Freeman's output became some of the most reported academic work on gentrification, landing news stories with headlines like "Studies: Gentrification a boost for everyone" and "Exploding the gentrification myth."[26]

24   Slater, Tom. "Missing Marcuse: On gentrification and displacement." *City* 13.2 (2009), 292–311; Duany, Andres. "Three cheers for gentrification: It helps revive cities and doesn't hurt the poor." *The American Enterprise*, April 2001, 37–39; Vigdor, Jacob L. "Does gentrification harm the poor?" *Brookings-Wharton Papers on Urban Affairs*, 2002, 133–82; McKinnish, Terra, Randall Walsh and T. Kirk White. "Who gentrifies low-income neighborhoods?" *Journal of Urban Economics* 67.2 (2010): 180–93; Kiviat, Barbara. "Gentrification: Not Ousting the Poor?" *Time*, June 29, 2008.

25   Freeman, Lance. *There goes the 'hood: Views of gentrification from the ground up.* Temple University Press, 2006.

26   Hampson, Rick. 2005. "Studies: Gentrification a boost for everyone." *USA Today*, April 20, 2005; Chamberlain, Lisa. "Exploding the gentrification myth." *New York Observer*, November 17, 2003.

Most planners are ultimately (and sometimes jubilantly) resigned to the idea that gentrification is a necessary outcome of urban change. From this standpoint, working class displacement is the price a city has to pay for improvements to neighborhood schools, parks, streets and housing. Robert Yaro, a longtime planner with New York's influential Regional Plan Association, represents this hand-wringing wing. In an interview with geographer Scott Larson, he characterized gentrification as "a real quandary. You preserve character and preserve the quality of life and people with money buy in, and people without are pushed out. How do you deal with that? Subsidies? Direct investment? New York has had a housing crisis since the 1940s. [Gentrification] is one of the constants, one of the results of the success of the city."[27]

Dan Doctoroff, who served as New York City's deputy mayor for economic development under Mayor Bloomberg and oversaw his redevelopment efforts, represents the unapologetic wing. Invoking his then-boss, Doctoroff once told a reporter, "As the Mayor says, 'if you want to solve the problem of gentrification, you should have crime go up, the schools get worse, the parks dirtier.' Gentrification is a natural product of market forces."[28] Under this school of thought, gentrification is an unassailable public good and a feature as basic to urban development as commerce is to capitalism.

In recent years, the hand-wringing approach seems to be winning out, with even boosters like Richard Florida waving

---

27   As quoted in Larson, Scott. *"Building like Moses with Jacobs in mind"*: *Contemporary planning in New York City.* Temple University Press, 2013, 24–25.
28   As quoted in Larson, *"Building like Moses with Jacobs in mind,"* 145.

the red flag and penning critiques of urban inequality.[29] Nonetheless, this viewpoint still sees gentrification as a symptom of success and often prescribes private development as its cure.

Taken together, these narratives—*highest and best use*, *value recapture*, *competitive advantage*, *creative class*, *livability* and *neighborhood effects*—represent some of the most potent ways planners legitimate displacement. They help reframe dispossession as development and popularize the notion that gentrification is something to be desired, not disparaged. Ultimately, according to these theories, gentrification is the outcome of good city planning.

Coercing Compliance

Beyond self-justification, planners are compelled by external forces to reshape their cities for investment. While real estate is a lead actor in cities' transformation, its costar is finance. By directing flows of money into and out of places and projects, banks and investors act as capitalists' own private planners. As economist J.W. Mason explains,

> the financial system is also where conscious planning takes its most fully developed form under capitalism. Banks are, in Schumpeter's phrase, the private equivalent of Gosplan, the Soviet planning agency. Their lending decisions determine what new projects will get a share of society's resources,

---

29 Florida, Richard. *The new urban crisis: How our cities are increasing inequality, deepening segregation, and failing the middle class—and what we can do about it.* Basic Books, 2017.

and suspend—or enforce—the "judgment of the market"
on money-losing enterprises.[30]

Property development is a big, intensive fixed-capital investment, and as such it requires enormous amounts of debt for both
the builder and the buyer. That capital is provided by banks,
which package bonds and mortgages into securities and sell
them off in pieces to investors. The result is a net of finance that
stretches across most of the world, and places enormous power
over city governance in the hands of financiers, bondholders
and debt speculators. Politicians and planners who try to challenge this historical bloc are frequently frustrated by its sheer
power and control, and those who persist are often punished.

In the international sphere, this disciplining usually comes
from global development organizations like the World Bank
and the International Monetary Fund (and, as in Chile or the
Congo, the CIA). On the local level, neoliberalism's enforcers
are much more banal: municipal credit rating agencies. Three
companies—Moody's, Standard & Poor's and Fitch Ratings—
control just about every city's ability to access capital through
the bond markets by grading them based on their likelihood
to repay their debts or default. These agencies look at each
city's economic mix, finances, debt level and management,
and they come to a decision about whether or not it is safe for
investment. As creatures of finance, they look for the markers of neoliberalism: a small state making limited expenditures
targeted at bringing in investment; public policies that support

30   Mason, J.W. "Socialize finance." *Jacobin*, November 28, 2016.

the FIRE sectors; weak unions, especially for public-sector workers; public-private partnerships to manage major urban projects; and business-friendly political regimes that fight the class war from the bankers' side. Where they find these traits, they mark a city as safe: AAA. Where they do not, the city's grade suffers.

Credit rating agencies are not hands-off investigators or passive reporters of economic prospects. They are ideologically driven activists who meet regularly with municipal governments in the United States and around the world to ensure capital's expanded reproduction. In New York, credit rating agencies rewarded the city for granting tax abatements and exemptions to developers in the 1980s, and for reducing benefits for government workers in the 1990s. In Detroit, despite the signs of an impending collapse of the city's primary industries, municipal credit ratings rose during the 1980s because its government was willing to pursue gentrification as a planning strategy. In the early 1990s, the city of Philadelphia was rewarded for a program of government shrinkage, municipal employee wage freezes and health care cuts. After improving the city's credit rating, Moody's wrote, "The only test for the city is to keep up the momentum."[31]

While many planners wish to opt out of this trap, they are left with few options. As federal spending on local projects declines, cities are on their own to pay for programs and close their budget gaps. Their ability to raise taxes is also often constrained by state and federal guidelines (as well as voters' will),

---

31   Hackworth, Jason. *The neoliberal city*, 37.

and they are legally prevented from deficit budgeting. The remaining vehicle is the bond market, and both the amount of bond issuances and their value has grown rapidly since the 1970s, with an especially sharp upturn from 2000 to 2010. Under these conditions, the consequences of a bad credit score can be severe. Not only will many private investors back away from poorly rated cities, but pension funds, money market funds and insurance companies—all major bondholders—generally will not invest in anything but top-graded bonds. The city that rejects gentrification planning is therefore taking a significant financial risk.

By choice or by force, planners use gentrification to create the physical environments for capital to thrive. It is the process by which cities seek capital, and capital seeks land. Its endgame is a city controlled by bankers and developers, run like a corporation, designed as a luxury product and planned by the finance sector. What was public becomes private; what was common becomes enclosed; what was cheap becomes expensive; what was shared becomes traded. Through the real estate state, the city becomes gentrified. Through gentrification, the city becomes neoliberal.

3

New York's Bipartisan Consensus

How has New York City planned in the twenty-first century? Is there a liberal and a conservative approach to gentrification planning?

There's a saying in the New York City tenant movement: real estate in New York is like oil in Texas. Not only is private property the city's biggest business, it's also its lifeblood. Like the oil fields of Texas, New York extracts value from its physicality: land, the skin of the city; buildings, its bones. Money flows through it as blood through the circulatory system. People enter like oxygen and are expelled like carbon dioxide. This is not a natural state, though; like all bodies under capitalism, it sells itself daily as a means of survival. As a result, real estate lurks behind every other major fight in the city, from labor struggles (which often cite rising housing costs as justification for higher wages) to environmental fights (which are often about who lives closest to noxious industries and toxic waste) to civil rights (which often center around both the right to move and "the right to stay put").[1]

---

1   Hartman, Chester. "The right to stay put." In Geisler, Charles and Frank Popper. *Land reform, American style*. Roman and Allanheld, 1984.

New York boosters sometimes call their city "the real estate capital of the world."[2] It has a limited amount of high-priced land, and its buildings hold exceedingly high property values. By 2016 its buildings and land were worth over $1 trillion, representing a hike of more than 10 percent over the previous year.[3] The real estate sector is the largest contributor to the New York metropolitan gross domestic product, one of the city's major employers and by far the largest donor to political campaigns. Between 2000 and 2016, real estate interests gave over $83 million to the state politicians who control New York City's rent and tax laws.[4] The city's campaign finance laws are stricter, but still contain loopholes that allow real estate fronts like "Jobs for New York" in 2013 and "Progress Now New York" in 2017 to donate millions. Both Republican and Democratic politicians depend on the real estate industry to maintain their governing and electoral coalitions, even if large segments of their constituencies—including tenants and small businesses—suffer at its expense.

In the twenty-first century, New York has been led by two mayors who, in many ways, could not be more different. Technocratic billionaire Michael Bloomberg, who was elected as a Republican before he became an independent, governed from 2002 through 2013. His rise was propelled by the growth of the city's "transnational capitalist" and "professional managerial" classes, and he spoke in their voice as an advocate for

2   Angotti, *New York for sale*.

3   David, Javier E. "NYC total property value surges over $1 trillion, setting record." *CNBC*, January 16, 2016.

4   Podkul, Cezary, Derek Kravitz and Will Parker. "Why developers of Manhattan luxury towers give millions to upstate candidates." *Pro Publica and The Real Deal*, December 30, 2016.

streamlined governance. Under his watch the city was managed as a "luxury product" to be sold, triggering an explosion of mega-developments and public-private partnerships.[5]

Democrat Bill de Blasio, who took office in 2014 and was reelected in 2017, presents himself as Bloomberg's opposite: a progressive populist who fights inequality and stands up for working class people of color. While he has pursued many policies that would have been anathema to Bloomberg, like paid sick leave and a higher minimum wage, he has also stimulated real estate development and raised land and property values through rezonings.

The story of New York in the early twenty-first century is one of continuity despite change. Conservative Michael Bloomberg and liberal Bill de Blasio are very different mayors, with divergent styles, priorities and coalitions. They both, however, are mayors of New York, capital city of the real estate state, and their planners are thus charged with the same mandate: to raise property values, promote development and encourage gentrification.

Bloomberg: Neoliberalism with New York Characteristics

Over the course of twelve years, Michael Bloomberg reshaped New York City in unprecedented ways. He was an unapologetic advocate for the rich, who, he argued, were key to the city's overall well-being. While he significantly altered the city's educational,

---

5 Brash, Julian. *Bloomberg's New York: Class and governance in the luxury city*. University of Georgia Press, 2011.

labor and environmental practices, the most visible upheaval was in the city's built environment. These changes were overseen by two planners: Dan Doctoroff, deputy mayor for economic development; and Amanda Burden, director of the Department of City Planning and chair of the City Planning Commission.

Doctoroff came out of finance. He worked for years as an analyst for Lehman Brothers, until he followed one of his clients, petro-billionaire and Trump associate Robert Bass, to the private equity firm Oak Hill Capital Partners. There, he became a specialist in real estate investment.

Burden's background was in planning and architecture. An heir to multiple fortunes, she worked at the architecture firm Gruzen & Partners and became a protégé of William "Holly" Whyte, the urban design critic and author of "The Case for Gentrification."[6] She went on to work for the New York State Urban Development Corporation and the Battery Park City Authority, where she helped run a massive public-private partnership and luxury real estate complex.

Throughout the city, Doctoroff, Burden and Bloomberg sparked a boom in "mega-developments," giant private construction projects with significant public backing. Many of these projects were linked back to an old obsession of Doctoroff's: a New York City Olympic bid.

On September 12, 2000, late in Rudy Giuliani's second term as mayor, a group calling itself NYC2012 presented a plan for New York to host the Olympic Games. Led by Doctoroff, NYC2012 called for a major round of new construction in

---

6 Whyte, *City*, 325–30.

working class and industrial neighborhoods. The Olympics would be an opportunity to portray New York as a global city, friendly to capital and tourism, and willing to dispense with the obsolete old in favor of the profitable new.

The group was composed of prominent landowners and government veterans. Doctoroff was an investor in several western Midtown properties; Roland Betts owned Chelsea Piers, a sports and entertainment complex, also on Manhattan's West Side; Lewis Rudin of Rudin Management was a leader in the city's real estate establishment; Daniel Rose ran Rose Associates, one of New York City's elite development firms with properties across Manhattan and plans for more in Long Island City and Downtown Brooklyn. Many of the other team members were experts in New York City government, with a particularly large number of Lindsay administration veterans.

The plan was ambitious. In Long Island City, they proposed an "Olympic village" to house visiting athletes and guests. In the south Bronx, they would build a velodrome and arena on industrial land and replace the existing Yankee Stadium with a new one nearby. In Downtown Brooklyn, they wanted a new stadium for basketball, volleyball and gymnastics. The plan's centerpiece was a redeveloped Midtown West, over and surrounding an active train yard. Under the plan, that area would see a $1.2 billion expansion of the Javits Convention Center, a new Madison Square Garden, an additional 72,000-seat stadium, several hotels and an eighty-story office tower. To accommodate this new growth, the 7 train—which crosses 42nd Street and stretches to Flushing, Queens—would be expanded further westward.

Giuliani signaled interest in the project and when Bloomberg was elected one year later he vigorously promoted the 2012 Olympics. Bloomberg immediately appointed Doctoroff as his deputy mayor for economic development, giving him oversight of the Department of City Planning, and several other members of NYC2012 were given influential positions.

The plan, however, was not terribly popular with New Yorkers. Though some embraced the Olympic excitement or looked forward to the jobs it might create, many believed the plan was designed more for the benefit of developers than residents. Stadiums had proven to be a failed economic development strategy in many other cities around the country and around the world, with Olympics being particularly destructive. Nonetheless, Bloomberg plowed forward.

In 2005, to many New Yorkers' relief, the Olympic Committee rejected the city's bid and chose London instead. The mayor and his allies were disappointed but not defeated. Bloomberg told reporters, "This effort was a catalyst for getting a lot of things going."[7] Indeed it was. One by one, the zombie projects rose from the dead, often in altered but recognizable forms.

The Queens Olympic Village plan was repackaged as an enormous middle- and upper-income housing complex in Long Island City, with 925 apartments and a waterfront park. The project is being developed by the Related Companies, whose senior advisor, Jay Kriegel, served as executive director of NYC2012 from 1997 through 2005.

---

7   Rutenberg, Jim. "Mayor says Olympic bid was worth a shot." *New York Times*, July 7, 2005.

The site of the proposed Bronx velodrome became a big box shopping complex, also developed by the Related Companies. Nearby, Yankee Stadium was rebuilt with massive public subsidies. The new stadium was placed on top of a public park where Bronx residents used to play pickup baseball.

A basketball stadium went up near Downtown Brooklyn and the project mushroomed under the auspices of the massive Atlantic Yards/Pacific Park development. Meanwhile, Downtown Brooklyn was transformed from the city's most active hub of Black-owned small businesses into a high-end, high-rise commercial and residential district.

Piece by piece, the 2012 Olympic bid transformed into a proliferation of mega-developments. Some of these projects were planned long before NYC2012; the Long Island City development, for example, had been a priority of the Koch, Dinkins and Giuliani administrations, but the money and political will never manifested to make it a reality. The Olympics served as a catalyst to mobilize planning imaginations and public and private money around a new form of urban renewal, which would put land to its "highest and best use" and unleash the "competitive advantage of the inner city."

As the mega-developments rose, a subtler but more profound transformation took place through land use policies. One of Bloomberg's lasting marks on the city was a massive, neighborhood-by-neighborhood rezoning offensive. Once completed, these changes would impact over 11,000 blocks—one third of the city's landmass—in forty-nine out of the city's fifty-nine community districts. The last time such a large-scale project was enacted was 1961, when the city's entire zoning code was overhauled, resulting in a spell of new high-rise construction and privately owned public spaces.

Bloomberg's rezonings, though vast in scale, cannot be mistaken for a comprehensive plan; they were in fact more of an abdication of planning to the market than a plan in and of themselves. Rezonings set limits for development and channeled it to certain places, but they rarely actually create new physical spaces or social policies. Zoning is less a plan than a parameter, a framework within which development does or does not take place.

Given the scope of New York City's rezonings between 2002 and 2013, and their overlap with the global financial boom and bust, it is difficult to generalize about their overall impact on the city. They simultaneously represented several contradictory tendencies, between preservation and new development, open space and density, "urban renewal" and "new urbanism." Most rezonings involved a mix of downzoning, upzoning and contextual zoning, choosing some parts of the neighborhood to defend and others to destroy.

In aggregate, however, there are trends. In 2010 the Furman Center for Real Estate and Urban Policy released a report on the rezonings' net impact on the city's housing capacity. Looking at the 188,000 residential lots that were rezoned from the start of 2003 to the end of 2007, the authors found that 14 percent were upzoned, 23 percent were downzoned and 63 percent were contextually zoned. The 14 percent of lots that were upzoned, however, accounted for 100 million square feet of new residential development capacity, or housing for about 200,000 new residents. Though most lots were contextually zoned, those that were upzoned created the potential for more new construction than the combined downzoning and contextual zonings protected.[8]

Though results varied by neighborhood and block, in its totality the Bloomberg rezonings reflected a particular racial capitalist spatial agenda: White upper-income homeowners tended to see their blocks downzoned or contextually zoned, while working class tenants of color tended to see their blocks upzoned. This pattern could not be explained away by any other obvious consideration. For example, transit access—the standard urban planning rationale for upzoning—did not seem to be a factor here, as 59 percent of downzoned lots were within half a mile of a subway entrance.[9]

This trend poses a peculiar economic logic. If the Bloomberg administration's planning priorities were geared toward making the city friendly to real estate and finance capital, why wouldn't it do just the opposite of what the data suggests and *upzone* wealthy White neighborhoods? Since property values in New York City are largely tied with land values, and upzoning tends to increase land values by raising the potential for development profit an owner can pursue, why wouldn't the Bloomberg administration reward its wealthier constituents with a lucrative upzoning?

The answer is politics. Bloomberg still had to win reelection (twice, it turned out), and his base demanded public policies that resulted in both elevated property values and increased "livability." Upzoning wealthy neighborhoods would have

---

8   Furman Center for Real Estate & Urban Policy. *How have recent rezonings affected the city's ability to grow?* New York University School of Law and Wagner School of Public Service, 2010.
9   Ibid.

further enriched many Bloomberg-supporting property owners, but they might not have wanted to stay in places like Park
Slope if their brownstone townhouses were suddenly over-
shadowed by construction cranes and glimmering skyscrapers.
Gentrification was already inflating their home values and so
quality of life planning was a higher priority for these voters
than an immediate economic stimulus. Meanwhile, developers
still benefited from the upzonings, which were often dramatic,
and they channeled their building energies toward the corri-
dors and corners the city selected.

Thus, planners were directed to protect many wealthy and
White neighborhoods, including most of Staten Island, with
preservationist policies and special zoning districts; in poorer
neighborhoods and communities of color, like much of Harlem, Bloomberg's planners rezoned to allow big development
projects to take root. Often planners took this approach within
the same rezoning. The Lower East Side/East Village rezoning of 2008, for example, helped preserve the most gentrified
parts of the area while upzoning its poorer blocks and leaving
most of Chinatown unprotected.

Citing neoclassical economics, city officials argued that
upzonings would increase the supply of housing in poorer areas,
sopping up demand and resulting in lower overall housing costs.
This argument, unfortunately, had little basis in reality. Late in
her term as planning commissioner, Amanda Burden admitted
as much. In a forum on urban growth, she told an audience:

I had believed that if we kept building in that manner and
increasing our housing supply ... that prices would go

down. We had every year almost 30,000 permits for housing, and we built a tremendous amount of housing, including affordable housing, either through incentives or through government funds. And the price of housing didn't go down at all. That's a practitioner's point of view. What we haven't figured out is the question of gentrification.[10]

This should not have come as a surprise. Simply adding housing supply does not necessarily drive down overall prices. In many cases, it does the opposite, since developers almost always build for the top of the market, not for the greatest need; real estate functions as plural—rather than singular—markets, meaning that increasing supply at the top of the market does nothing to reduce demand at the bottom; purchasers of luxury housing often do not live there full time, thereby creating an enormous market for empty apartments; people generally do not move frequently, so the kind of "self-sorting" required for residents to meet their "market equilibrium" does not actually take place; and in the absence of tight and universal rent controls, the rise of big flashy buildings is more likely to raise than diminish neighbors' rents. Because luxury real estate is such a reliable and under-taxed investment in New York City, it is exceedingly rare for tall new buildings in gentrifying neighborhoods to rent or sell at rates that are affordable to those who live nearby. In most cases, they are the kinds of luxury projects that result in displacement—either directly through demolition, or indirectly by elevating rents in the surrounding area.

---

10   Goodyear, Sarah. "'What we haven't figured out yet is the question of gentrification.'" *City Lab*, October 8, 2013.

To compensate for this fact, and in response to campaigns by nonprofit housing advocates and developers, Bloomberg's planners would often allow a voluntary "inclusionary housing" bonus in new developments, whereby a developer could build 20 percent more than the zoning would otherwise permit if they set aside 20 percent of the apartments at a lower cost. But 20 percent is not a lot of value to recapture, and as practiced most of these "affordable" apartments are out of the price range of most neighborhood residents. This only results in another form of gentrification, rather than a real solution to the city's low-cost housing shortage.

Bloomberg's zoning changes reflected a double standard in the city's policies regarding housing and the market. On poor blocks, planners leaned on the market to solve the housing crisis and used zoning as the catalyst for new development. On rich blocks, planners used zoning as an anti-market force, holding back the spread of new development for the benefit of current residents.

Over twelve years, Mayor Bloomberg's Department of City Planning proposed 123 rezonings; 122 of them passed. This is not because they were overwhelmingly popular. Many rezonings, from Jamaica, Queens, to West Harlem, were protested by residents and rejected by their community boards—the supposed gatekeepers of local land use decisions—only to be approved by the city council and mayor at the end of the review process. Public input is sought on all of these projects, but their feedback is nonbinding. Other than the mayor and the City Planning Commission (the majority of which is handpicked by the mayor and is dominated by real estate professionals) the real player in a rezoning is the city council member representing the district in question. It is legislative custom in New York, as in most US cities, for the entire city council to vote with the local representative on land use decisions; they are then expected to reciprocate the favor when the time comes. For the mayor to ensure victory, then, all that is really needed is one crucial vote. Once secured, either through political favors or promises of benefits for the district, the rezoning is virtually assured approval.

The one case in which a city-sponsored rezoning was thwarted was Kingsbridge Armory in the central Bronx. There, Bloomberg's Department of City Planning proposed building a mall inside a historic military building, to be developed by the Related Companies. Negotiations broke down over the issue of securing a living wage for future mall employees, and when enough unions and community-based organizations turned against the project, the Bronx Council delegation opposed the project as well. When the rezoning went before the city council, just one member—a lame duck conservative Democrat from Jackson Heights—voted in support of the project. A revised plan to convert the armory into a high-end ice skating rink is now in motion, this time with the support of the local power brokers.

The Bronx armory was the exception that proves the rule, a rare case when the growth coalition fell apart at the last minute. Literally 99 percent of the time, the Department of City Planning ensured that development was channeled in the way it saw fit: big development in working class areas, neighborhood enhancements in wealthy neighborhoods and gentrification in every place that could support it.

De Blasio: "Progressive Activist, Fiscal Conservative"

After twelve years of Bloomberg, New Yorkers were ready for a change. Fueled by the energy of Occupy Wall Street and the movements against police racism and brutality, Public Advocate Bill de Blasio ran a surprisingly effective candidacy that highlighted economic inequality as its defining issue. De Blasio handily swept his better-known primary contenders and then trounced his Republican opponent in the general election with 73 percent of the vote. The Bloomberg days were definitively done.

The de Blasio candidacy, however, displayed some deep contradictions. He decried the "tale of two cities" that had characterized Bloomberg's time in office, but he could never quite explain why he had supported some of Bloomberg's most egregious gentrification plans during his tenure as a Brooklyn city councilmember. In a campaign speech before the Association for a Better New York, a corporate lobbying group that emerged from the city's 1975 bankruptcy and continues to push for a combination of austerity and gentrification, de Blasio characterized himself a "progressive activist, fiscal conservative" without explaining what, exactly, that might mean.[11]

Both as a candidate and mayor, de Blasio plainly stated that he "has a critique of the free enterprise system" and believes in a more planned society. In a particularly elaborate version of this line, he told a reporter:

---

11 Engquist, Erik. "De Blasio calls himself a 'fiscal conservative.'" *Crain's New York Business*, October 4, 2013.

What's been hardest is the way our legal system is structured to favor private property. I think people all over this city, of every background, would like to have the city government be able to determine which building goes where, how high it will be, who gets to live in it, what the rent will be. I think there's a socialistic impulse, which I hear every day, in every kind of community, that they would like things to be planned in accordance to their needs. And I would, too. Unfortunately, what stands in the way of that is hundreds of years of history that have elevated property rights and wealth to the point that that's the reality that calls the tune on a lot of development.[12]

This vision could not be more different than Bloomberg's; de Blasio's governing approach to planning, real estate and development, however, was quite similar. At the start of his first term, two appointments foreshadowed what was to come: Carl Weisbrod as director of the Department of City Planning and chair of the City Planning Commission; and Alicia Glen as deputy mayor for housing and economic development.

Weisbrod had a long career blending real estate and planning. Though he began as a tenant lawyer, his tenure in government started in the Lindsay administration's displacement unit, euphemistically known as the "Department of Relocation." Under Koch, he led the effort to Disneyfy and gentrify Times Square. Under Dinkins, he founded the Economic Development

---

12   Smith, Chris. "In conversation: Bill de Blasio." *New York Magazine*, September 4, 2017.

Corporation—a group controlled by the mayor and the corporate lobbying organization Partnership for New York City—that matches private developments with public subsidies. Under Bloomberg, he ran the Lower Manhattan Development Corporation, which, after 9/11, channeled federal funding into private real estate projects. At the same time, he managed Trinity Church's immense real estate holdings and worked as a land use lobbyist at the powerful consultancy HR&A. Weisbrod frequently professes his belief that real estate is a social good; as he once told reporters, "There are very few industries where the self-interest of the industry and the fundamental interests of the citizens of the city are so deeply intertwined as the real estate industry."[13] By choosing Weisbrod as commissioner, de Blasio signaled that planning and real estate would remain thoroughly "intertwined."

Deputy Mayor Alicia Glen was straight out of Goldman Sachs, where she ran the Urban Investment Group and channeled finance into gentrifying working class neighborhoods through "social impact bonds." For example, Glen financed the Kalahari condominium project in East Harlem, a luxury high-rise that also included some "affordable" apartments for households making 185 percent of the area median income (AMI)—a calculation that already skews well above the citywide average income because it includes several surrounding suburban counties. According to Glen, the project "was really groundbreaking, because nobody before has thought that somebody would spend $1 million to buy an apartment in a building [where] other people could buy

---

13   Schlanger, Danielle. "Brod outlook: Carl Weisbrod on revitalizing Midtown East and making NYC affordable." *Commercial Observer*, April 8, 2015.

[one] for $200,000."[14] Though Glen's position had previously been titled "deputy mayor for economic development," de Blasio threw the word "housing" into her title, suggesting that Glen was picked for her acuity in financializing the home.

De Blasio, Weisbrod and Glen's defining planning initiative was entitled *Housing New York: A Five-Borough, Ten-Year Plan*. Released just months after his election, the mayor called it one of "the strongest, most progressive affordable housing policies in the nation."[15] With a $41 billion price tag and a promise to build 80,000 new units of affordable housing and preserve 120,000 currently affordable units, it would "change the face of this city forever" as "the largest, fastest affordable housing plan ever attempted at a local level."[16] Given its emphasis on affordability, the plan struck many New Yorkers as a bold left jab at Bloomberg's legacy of gentrification zoning and luxury mega-developments.

Like any big city plan, *Housing New York* contains many elements: a promise to continue nonprofit funding for low-income and supportive housing; a series of tweaks to the zoning code that encourage slightly bigger buildings in contextually zoned districts; a commitment to extend subsidies on existing affordable housing; and a series of upzonings that would be tied to the creation of new, income-targeted "affordable" housing.

---

14   Smith, Stephen J. "Shades of Bloomberg in New York's next housing czar." *Next City*, December 27, 2013.

15   Durkin, Erin. "De Blasio, City Council strike deal on support for affordable housing plan." *Daily News*, March 14, 2016.

16   Fermino, Jennifer. "Mayor de Blasio unveils $41B proposal to develop 200,000 units of affordable housing." *Daily News*, March 4, 2014. In the run-up to his reelection, de Blasio would revise these figures to $43 billion for 120,000 units of construction and 180,000 units of preservation. Though the numbers changed, the assumptions remained the same.

It was that last policy—known as "mandatory inclusionary housing" (MIH)—that would define the mayor's housing and development agenda moving forward.

"Inclusionary zoning" was not new to New York City. Ed Koch created the voluntary "density bonus" (or geobribe) in 1987 and Bloomberg used it to gain popular support for many of his 122 rezonings. By de Blasio's time, however, the program had come under attack for two reasons.

First, it failed to produce much affordable housing. As a voluntary program, developers could take it or leave it, and more often than not they chose the latter. With the exception of two neighborhoods—Williamsburg and Manhattan's West Side—most developers were perfectly happy to build as much as the city allowed and charge full rents. When they chose to participate, many elected to build their below market housing "off sight" in faraway neighborhoods, or contribute to the city's affordable housing fund instead.

Second, the "affordable" housing was often wildly unaffordable to current neighborhood residents, or those most in need of shelter. Most of the new apartments were reserved for households making 80 percent of AMI, or $66,000 when de Blasio came to office. Because the AMI includes so many suburban counties, it is significantly higher than the city's median income. Eighty percent of New York City's median income would have been just $39,000. In the neighborhoods targeted for upzoning, median incomes are often far lower.[17]

---

17   Dulchin, Benjamin, Moses Gates and Barika Williams. "Housing policy for a strong and equitable city." In Mollenkopf, John and Brad Lander (eds) *Toward a 21st century for all: Progressive policies for New York City for*

If the critique of inclusionary zoning in New York City was that it produced too few apartments at too high rents, then the solution seemed obvious: planners should force more developers to participate, and with better income targets. At first glance, that's exactly what de Blasio did. Rather than a voluntary bonus, MIH made income-targeted housing a requirement. Rather than focusing on 80 percent AMI, the program promises housing for those making as little as 40 percent AMI. The de Blasio program promised to recapture a whole lot more value than the Bloomberg approach.

Look a little deeper, however, and the problems become clearer. Yes, the program includes one option in which 20 percent of new buildings must be set aside for those making 40 percent AMI ($42,000 for a family of four), but it also includes other formulas. In one of them, developers can build for households making 115 percent AMI ($115,000). That option is for what they call "emerging markets," language developed by World Bank official Antoine van Agtmael in 1981 to describe countries that had undergone structural adjustment.[18] There is no provision for households making 30 percent of AMI ($31,000), which is where the city's real need lies. This group includes minimum wage workers, average single mother-led households, most of the people on public housing waiting lists and seniors on fixed

---

2013 and beyond. Center for Urban Research, City University of New York, 2013. These figures are rounded to the nearest thousand. The exact figures: 80% of area median income is $66,400; 80% of city median income is $38,994. New York City Housing Preservation and Development. "Affordability and Area Median Income (AMI)." 2018.

18   Prashad, Vijay. *The poorer nations: A possible history of the global south*. Verso Books, 2013, 173.

incomes.[19] Fifty-seven percent of Black and 62 percent of Latino New Yorkers earn less than the plan's income targets and are thus functionally excluded from this housing.[20]

While the program is mandatory, it is unevenly distributed. Rather than blanketing the entire city, MIH only kicks in where the city upzones. This means that the actual number of income-targeted units the program creates depends on the success or failure of many different individual neighborhood rezonings. Greater affordable housing production is therefore not guaranteed.

The real problem with this plan, though, is not the precise rent levels or the number of units, but rather the model's organizing logic: in order to be successful, the plan must marshal a multitude of rich people into places that are already experiencing gentrification. MIH was supposed to create 16,000 apartments for families making $42,000—just 3 percent of the need for such apartments in the city today, according to the plan's own figures. At the same time, it would add 100,000 luxury apartments to these same neighborhoods. As Rob Robinson, co-founder of Take Back the Land, argues, "any model like that only saturates New York City with market-rate housing."[21]

---

19 Williams, Barika. "Who's left out if we don't serve 30 percent AMI." Association for Neighborhood & Housing Development blog, March 9, 2016. These figures are rounded to the nearest thousand. The exact figures are: 40% of area median income for a family of four is $41,720; 115% of AMI is $114,730; 30% of AMI is 31,290.

20 Durkin, Erin. "Majorities of Black and Latino families make too little to qualify for de Blasio's affordable housing plan, analysis finds." *New York Daily News*, March 3, 2016.

21 Robinson, Rob. "NYC housing advocates and the global struggle." *City Limits*, March 20, 2015.

Unless targeted toward wealthy areas—and thus far the opposite has been true—the results are predictable: once the rich arrive, rent gaps will appear in the surrounding area; landlords will seek to close them through rent hikes and evictions; neighborhood stores will close; more working class people will be displaced by gentrification than will ever be housed in the new inclusionary complexes; a few somewhat-affordable apartments will be built in neighborhoods that are suddenly and severely transformed.

At the same time, this version of inclusionary zoning could incentivize developers to destroy actually existing affordable housing. Many New York City neighborhoods are filled with rent-regulated apartments, often built at lower densities than the new inclusionary zoning rules permit. When planners upzone neighborhoods to allow bigger buildings, rent-stabilized landlords will have every reason to sell their properties to speculative developers, who could then knock down the existing properties and build something bigger and more expensive. A percentage of the new building would be affordable, but the outcome would likely be a net loss in low-cost apartments and a major hit to the rent-regulated housing stock. Raquel Namuche of the Ridgewood Tenants Union notes, "we're creating affordable housing units, but at the same time we're also losing many rent-stabilized apartments. If you don't do enough to protect people's rights to their apartments, then what are you actually doing?"[22]

22　Fang, Benjamin. " Tenant activists call for de Blasio's resignation." *Forest Hills/Rego Park Times*. January 17, 2017.

When confronted with the ways the plan could encourage gentrification, Glen responded, "We have certain tools in our municipal tool box. We can't change the entire history of capitalism and we're not Trotsky. You try to redistribute some of that growth to the people that need it." This, of course, assumes that what people in need *need* is more real estate development. In this same unusually frank interview, she claimed that

> [t]he reason why so many people are pissed [about the plan] is that they have been conditioned to the fear of change. I don't like it when my dry cleaner changes ownership. It pisses me off because I've known those people for years. It stresses me out. I don't like change. But change is inevitable and so how you shape the future is incredibly important as opposed to letting it wash over you. Because it's coming.[23]

In other words: this is capitalism and we are capitalists; mass displacement is equivalent to a dry cleaning management change; gentrification is inevitable; and people should just shut up already.

While some free-marketers at the Manhattan Institute and the *New York Post* pushed back against de Blasio's zoning plan, developers largely lined up in support. They wanted to stay on the mayor's good side, of course, but they also knew a deal when they saw one. City Hall's press release announcing the proposal came with a ringing endorsement from Steven

---

23　Moskowitz, Peter. "Can New York save itself from out-of-control rents?" *Vice*, November 8, 2015.

Spinola, then president of the Real Estate Board of New York and one of the most powerful lobbyists in the state. It also included praise from Bill Rudin, chairman of the Association for a Better New York and a developer whose company was responsible for converting St. Vincent's Hospital into a luxury condo complex; opposing that development was a centerpiece of de Blasio's first mayoral campaign.

These developers knew that even the anticipation of a rezoning could spark speculation and result in higher profits. Such was the case for East New York, the first neighborhood to undergo an inclusionary upzoning under de Blasio. East New York was a telling choice: it was a textbook example of a redlined, disinvested and blockbusted neighborhood, and it had remained Black and working class while much of the rest of the borough became Whiter and richer. Between 2000 and 2010, as Brooklyn's Black population fell by 6 percent, East New York's rose by 13 percent as those displaced by gentrification relocated to this last affordable section.[24]

What the de Blasio plan did, however, was signal that public policy would soon change the market calculus and help the neighborhood realize its "highest and best use." In a land market like New York's, the mere prospect of an upzoning—even if premised on mandatory affordable housing—is enough to set off a speculative frenzy. In anticipation, speculators bought and sold East New York land and property at an incredible

---

24 Tepper, Joseph and Erin Durkin. "Black population surges in East New York as it falls across the borough and city." *Daily News*, May 10, 2012.

clip, sending land prices up 63 percent.[25] This, in turn, caused rents to rise 16 percent to an average of $1,850. This would be "affordable" for a household earning $74,000; average incomes in East New York, however, are just $32,000. City comptroller Scott Stringer calculated that this level of speculation put 55 percent of the population at risk of displacement.[26]

Whereas Michael Bloomberg could have written off such changes as signs of progress, de Blasio could not. A key component of his base is working class African Americans and immigrants, who are the most adversely affected by these changes and who have led movements against gentrification in their neighborhoods. Such organizing has recently secured a number of important victories, including a "right to council" for low-income tenants, a two-year rent freeze for rent-stabilized renters and a number of new anti-harassment laws. From this vantage point, some have argued that de Blasio represents a break with growth machine politics. Making these concessions, however, has not stopped de Blasio from pursuing further upzonings in working class areas of the city. In fact, some of these new initiatives, like the "certificate of non-harassment" program and funding for tenant-initiated legal actions, are geographically linked to rezonings and therefore act as sweeteners for the bitter high-end development plans. De Blasio's palliative efforts have immediately helped many renters, but

---

25   Savich-Lew, Abigail. "Some suspect East New York rezoning has triggered speculation." *City Limits*, March 10, 2016.

26   Stringer, Scott. "Mandatory inclusionary housing and the East New York rezoning: An analysis." *Office of the New York City Comptroller*, December 2, 2015.

his major planning policy will worsen the housing crisis in the long run by fueling speculation and driving up land and property values.

As de Blasio's planners were forcefully arguing for upzonings in working class neighborhoods, they were quietly unloading public assets onto big developers and private equity landlords. The largest of these giveaways was "NextGen NYCHA," a plan to encourage private construction on public housing land. De Blasio did not invent this idea; Bloomberg had tried a similar scheme at the end of his third term, but was shut down by resident opposition. Nor is de Blasio responsible for the housing authority's $100 million operating budget deficit and $17 billion in unmet maintenance costs; HUD has been underfunding the agency for over thirty-five years. What de Blasio did, though, was couch these privatizations as a pillar of his progressive vision.

Under NextGen, the public land surrounding public housing that is currently used for playgrounds, parking, or open space could be leased to private developers. Much of the new housing would be at least half luxury, and the rest "affordable" for families making 60 percent of AMI (or roughly $52,000 for a family of four). The average New York City Housing Authority (NYCHA) household, however, makes just $23,300. The new housing would therefore diminish public housing residents' public spaces, and replace them with private housing most cannot afford. The plan also calls for accelerating a transfer of public housing complexes over to private management through programs like the federal Rental Assistance Demonstration (RAD) program. Under RAD, private for-profit managers take over public housing and are immediately eligible for all sorts of financing that public housing authorities cannot access. While de Blasio's NextGen plan was not a wholesale privatization of public housing, it put NYCHA on that path. Among public housing residents, the plan was quickly redubbed "NextGentrification."

NextGen was presented to the public as a desperate measure for desperate times: a way to turn NYCHA's greatest financial asset—its high-value landholdings—into a means to confront its greatest liability—its enormous budget deficit. It turns out, however, that infill development would not actually generate much income. De Blasio plans to lease the first infill site, on a playground on the northern edge of the Upper East Side, to a private developer for a onetime fee of $25 million. That fee, however, would permanently buy the developer off paying city property taxes and make them eligible for $13 million in subsidies. In exchange for this public housing playground, then, the city would net just $12 million, a drop in the bucket compared to its $17 billion maintenance needs.[27]

Nevertheless, the plan moves forward. De Blasio's first NYCHA chair, Shola Olatoye, called on the Trump administration to relax federal regulations in order to speed up private construction. In a conversation with reporters, she rhetorically asked, "Can we use the, shall we say, bias of this administration towards the private sector, towards deregulation to help us? Absolutely, and we should." In that letter, she called on

---

27   Smith, Greg B. "Developer who won NYCHA building bid is de Blasio donor: records." *Daily News*, May 18, 2017.

HUD to "align with private housing industry practices to increase efficiency and further public-private partnerships."[28] In the meantime, NYCHA garnered renewed public scrutiny, when—on top of worsening conditions generally—it was discovered that the agency had been concealing its negligence in lead paint testing. Between 2012 and 2016, at least 1,160 children under six years old living in public housing suffered from lead poisoning.[29] The agency is now under a federal consent decree—a move that, ironically, could hasten the flow of private capital.

Beyond public housing, the de Blasio administration scoured their public holdings for private development opportunities. As with de Blasio's NYCHA program, this practice was not new; the city has been shedding public assets since at least the 1980s. What was noteworthy was its scope, scale and framing. According to a source who worked in the Land Use Planning unit of the NYC Department of Citywide Administrative Services (DCAS), de Blasio's DCAS commissioner instructed agency staffers to locate every single scrap of city-owned land that could be developed or have its air rights sold, often with the stated goal of meeting the mayor's housing metrics.

Sometimes the city simply gave away its land. In his first three years, the de Blasio administration orchestrated a concerted transfer of public land to private, often for-profit, developers: over 202 publicly owned vacant lots were "sold"

---

28 De La Hoz, Felipe. "Under Trump, a potential silver lining for NYCHA." *Gotham Gazette*, August 24, 2017.
29 Smith, Greg B. "Number of lead poisoned children in NYC public housing now tops 1,100." *Daily News*, August 30, 2018.

for $1.[30] These handovers were joined by a policy of selling "restricted deeds," or legal covenants the city placed on public buildings when they transferred ownership to private operators. These deeds mandated a certain type of use for the buildings, such as "community facilities." At the city's discretion, however, private operators can buy out these deeds and do with the land whatever the zoning will allow, or whatever a zoning variance would provide. These property transfers and regulatory derelictions helped facilitate the rapid disintegration of New York City's public and community spaces.

For example, in November 2016, de Blasio's DCAS sold the deed restriction for a property owned by the Dance Theater of Harlem, which would have restricted the lot to a cultural use. At a cost of $875,000, however, the owners could then sell the building to a developer, who could in turn build luxury housing. In this case, the $3.1 million buyer was BRP Companies, a developer that had recently donated to de Blasio's nonprofit fund, the Campaign for One New York.[31]

That same week, DCAS sold the deed on Rivington House, a Lower East Side health clinic that specialized in AIDS hospice care. The building's owner, VillageCare, sought to sell the building to Allure Group, which promised to operate the site as a for-profit nursing home. VillageCare's lobbyist, a major de Blasio donor, secured a deal that would invalidate the deed restriction for $16.5 million. Soon thereafter, Allure Group

---

30   Dovey, Rachel. "Mapping all of the NYC lots sold for a dollar." *Next City*, March 6, 2018.

31   Goodman, David J. "Builder acquires valuable Harlem plot after deed change." *New York Times*, May 13, 2016.

flipped the building for $116 million to a conglomerate of condominium developers, which included China's largest developer, Vanke.[32]

While these deed sales caught the attention of tabloids and federal prosecutors, another set of shady deals remained largely outside the public view. These were not about new development, but rather the promised "preservation" of 180,000 currently affordable apartments. To reach that number, the mayor's team—lead by Glen—negotiated a series of transactions between owners and buyers of large subsidized and rent-stabilized housing complexes.

In the case of subsidized housing—private buildings that received federal, state or city money to rent at lower costs—these deals extended public funding into the future. Often, however, planners used programs like Article XI of the state's Private Housing Finance Law to target future rentals toward people with much higher incomes than those who previously lived in these developments. Most of the "affordable" housing preserved during de Blasio's first term would rent for $2,500 per month—hardly affordable to most subsidized housing tenants.[33]

In the case of rent-stabilized buildings, the city structured several convoluted deals between building owners and private equity buyers. The 11,250-unit Stuyvesant Town was sold to the world's biggest landlord, the private equity firm Blackstone. As part of the package, the city provided Blackstone

---

32 Goodman, David J. "How New York allowed gentrification for $16 million." *New York Times*, March 30, 2016.

33 Real Affordability for All. "Increasing real affordability in New York City: An action plan for Mayor de Blasio's second term." September 2017.

with $221 million in giveaways, from tax breaks to 0 percent interest loans to transferable air rights, and in exchange asked them to keep some already expensive apartments stabilized.[34] Harlem's 1,229-unit Rivington complex, which was built as the Black counterpart to the Whites-only Stuyvesant Town, was sold to A&E Real Estate Holdings. The deal gave A&E over $100 million in tax breaks, and included a commitment to invest $40 million in the property—investments that entitle the new owner to big, permanent rent increases.[35] The deal at the nearby 1,790-unit Savoy Park was even worse. There, Fairstead Capital bought sixteen rent-stabilized buildings for $315 million, a price that could not be profitable without widespread evictions and rent increases. In fact, the terms of the deal allow 800 apartments to see nearly $1,000 a month rent increases.[36] Through these transactions, de Blasio's planners helped put affordable housing in the hands of some of the biggest, worst landlords in the game, gave them plenty of incentives to raise rents, then celebrated victory toward "preserving" thousands of affordable apartments.

With deals like these, it's no wonder many real estate leaders love this liberal mayor almost as much as his conservative predecessor. When it comes to land use and housing, de Blasio's team has carried on many of the city's real estate-friendly past practices and called it progress.

34 Sweeting, Kevin. "How Stuy Town got a tourniquet while Blackstone gets billions." *Gothamist*, March 31, 2016.

35 Brenzel, Kathryn. "A&E Real Estate buys Riverton housing complex for $201M." *The Real Deal*, December 17, 2015.

36 Maurer, Mark. "Fairstead in contract to buy 1,800-unit Savoy Park in Harlem." *The Real Deal*, February 25, 2016.

Whatever the Problem, the Solution is Luxury Development

New York's past two mayors are not one and the same. They represent different ideologies, different values, different priorities and different coalitions. But no matter how different they may be, and no matter how divergent their paths to city hall and the visions they have charted, a few constants remain. Both trusted a tight group of advisors and remained guarded with the press. Both believed in a bigger and stronger police force, and encouraged crackdowns on homeless people and other "quality of life" offenders. Finally, they both subscribed to the same planning paradigm: whatever the problem, the solution is luxury development.

Housing is too expensive? Both Bloomberg and de Blasio claimed that their massive upzonings would provide affordable housing to New Yorkers and solve the perpetual housing crisis. The only catch was that all the new affordable apartments would be accompanied by dramatic increases in luxury apartments. As those skyscrapers rose, rents rose alongside them. Tellingly, so did vacancies: between 2014 and 2017, 69,000 new units of housing were built in New York City; during the same period, 63,000 additional apartments went vacant.[37] Almost all of the growth in housing was eaten by emptiness—either incidentally, as in the rare cases of apartments that simply will not rent or sell, or intentionally, as in

---

37 New York City Department of Housing Preservation and Development, "Selected initial findings of the 2017 New York City Housing and Vacancy Survey," February 9, 2018. These figures are rounded to the nearest thousand. The exact figures are: 69,147 new units were produced while 62,854 went vacant.

the far more common cases of Airbnbs, pied-à-terres and pure investment vehicles.

Can't fund public housing? While the federal government starved public housing for decades, these two mayors sought to address this failing by providing new private investment and development opportunities. Both Bloomberg and de Blasio's signature solution to this crisis was to lease projects to banks and build luxury housing on NYCHA land. As a result, public housing residents feel even less secure in their tenure and even more squeezed in by the rich.

Worried about jobs? The long transition from a diverse economy to a real estate state implies changes not just for capital, but also for labor. A great many New Yorkers' jobs are closely connected with the ebb and flow of real estate investment, whether they are employed in construction, renovation, demolition, maintenance, security, cleaning, hospitality, sales or finance. This means that mayors sell every development as a jobs program. Bloomberg and de Blasio successfully recruited strong backing from organized labor, which publicly celebrated their plans in return for promises of contracts and jobs. This support came less from building trades unions—classic members of the "urban growth machine"—than the more politically savvy service and municipal unions (such as the Service Employees International Union, the Hotel Trades Council, and the American Federation of State, County and Municipal Employees).

Insufficient transportation? Since the Rapid Transit Act of 1894, the city's pursuit of better transit has always triggered speculation. In recent years, however, the linkage has become more explicit. In the city's first subway extension in twenty-six years, Bloomberg convinced the Metropolitan Transit Authority to extend the 7 line to his Hudson Yards development, and to pay for floated bonds based on the increased tax revenue from rising nearby property values. One of de Blasio's main transportation initiatives, a streetcar that would snake along the Brooklyn-Queens waterfront, uses the same funding trick. The plan only works if the already transformed waterfront undergoes an even more severe gentrification.

Need new parks? Many of the city's newest parks are closely tied to real estate schemes. Brooklyn Bridge Park is financed through the conversion of nearby piers and warehouses into luxury housing. The celebrated High Line is funded by a private conservancy, which in turn is funded by donations from developers and property owners along the route. This is not a totally new phenomenon; Central Park was also financed through a tax on increased property values along its borders. But the model is back with a vengeance, and new park spaces are increasingly treated as amenities for luxury development.

The land is polluted? When and how the city's toxic sites are remediated has everything to do with real estate values. Under Bloomberg and de Blasio, New York City's municipal brownfield program allocates its funds like a capitalist firm: based on the expectation of a return on investment. Remediation thus occurs as a first step toward luxury development. In places like Staten Island's North Shore, for example, local residents are caught in a quandary: their land is polluted and it's hurting them every day; the only plan on offer, however, links cleanup to large-scale luxury development, which threatens to displace them.[38]

Schools are struggling? New York City public schools are a mixed bag: some offer challenging curricula and encourage intellectual independence, while others subordinate learning to militaristic discipline. Both Bloomberg and de Blasio made education reform a priority, and both linked public school success to the problem of racial and economic segregation. Their gentrification plans became means to diversify public schools and maximize "neighborhood effects": new luxury development in poor neighborhoods is supposed to bring about "equity and opportunity" for all students. This does not always work out, since there are numerous ways for wealthier parents in gentrifying neighborhoods to steer their children out of their traditional neighborhood school: charters, magnets, private schools and even fraud are all common tactics. Working class kids are then stuck in segregated schools while their parents' rents rise.

Neighborhoods are segregated? A cursory look at the data on racial change in New York City shows that during the Bloomberg era, upzoned neighborhoods became more racially diverse. De Blasio amplified Bloomberg's zoning policies, so the same results should be expected. The key to understanding this data, however, is that most of this change was accomplished by

---

38   Checker, Melissa. "Green is the new black: 'Old school toxics' and environmental gentrification on a New York City waterfront." In Isenhour, Cindy, Gary McDonogh and Melissa Checker. *Sustainability in the global city: Myth and practice*. Cambridge University Press, 2015.

building expensive housing in historically Black, Latino and Asian neighborhoods. While these administrations argued that they were undoing redlining and ghettoization, it was a one-way integration process, and it went the wrong way: displacing people of color from areas where they had built power, rather than integrating segregated White neighborhoods.

Arts need a boost? As the city gets more expensive, it ceases to be a place where artists of all sorts can live, and therefore loses some of the vitality that makes it appealing in the first place. At the same time, artists can be useful in the gentrification process, doing the hard work of loft conversion and gallery opening, only to be kicked out when rents rise. Artists are on both sides of the gentrification fight, and can therefore be played by politicians seeking to beautify their luxury developments. Under Bloomberg, that meant including arts spaces in public-private mega-developments and neighborhood rezonings, and using construction walls like those at Atlantic Yards to display local artwork. Under de Blasio, it meant hiring real estate consultancies that had worked on MIH rezonings and the Brooklyn-Queens streetcar proposal to craft the administration's "comprehensive cultural plan." In both cases, the solution to a priced-out arts scene was pricey real estate.

Want to preserve African burial grounds? In perhaps the most absurd variation on this theme, New York City is proposing mixed-use development as a way to protect desecrated African burial grounds. In East Harlem, a seventeenth-century Dutch cemetery for free and enslaved Africans was covered over and developed, eventually becoming a bus depot. After a ground-swell of protest, the city's Economic Development Corporation and the local councilmember proposed that a memorial be built, and funded by an adjacent development that would include hundreds of apartments, a parking lot and an office building. In order to redress the harm caused by developing over an African burial ground, the city is now planning to develop over that same African burial ground.

No matter the question, the answer is the same. The pattern holds under a liberal and a conservative administration, suggesting something much bigger than the figure at the top of the political pyramid. Politicians come and go; coalitions join together and fall apart; but throughout it all, this strategy—planning through real estate—remains.

Planners rely on real estate for two reasons. First, because real estate is by far the most powerful player in the market. As in many other cities, landlords and developers control New York City and state politicians, they fund the local media and they dominate the Planning Commission. Second, in this private land market, real estate capitalists absorb any land improvements that planners design. If they are going to benefit anyway, they become "stakeholders" who must be involved in any planning decision. The fastest way to get their buy-in is to give them an opportunity to build.

Some planners play this game earnestly and believe that encouraging luxury development will generate more tax revenue for the public good (despite the tax breaks they use to incentivize development), or that increased supply will cause overall prices to drop (even though this kind of sorting rarely takes place in the real world). Others do so cynically, knowing planning through real estate will not work but will please their bosses and their bosses' patrons. Still others do not like it at all, but see no other alternative on the horizon and are commanded by policy elites to push for perpetual construction. Given cities' dependency on landowners, these civil servants—who tend to remain in place even as administrations change—are tasked with anchoring municipal governments to the interests of developers and landlords.

In this capitalist democracy, planners make the real estate market, but they cannot control it. Because they have encouraged such an oversupply, the luxury real estate market may be beginning to dip. In New York and elsewhere, high-end condominium sales have slowed, and prices have begun to drop at the very top. New capital controls imposed in China could limit the amount of foreign luxury purchases, and uncertainty caused by the erratic Trump administration may make otherwise interested investors balk. More existentially, climate change threatens to make the whole stretches of urban coastline uninhabitable and valueless.

Even as the market shows signs of stress, the push for development has not diminished. In fact, if the market tumbles, planners and politicians will likely respond by providing even more generous subsidies to luxury developers, since most of their planning strategies rely on a booming real estate market. They also know that under the right conditions, declining investment in property can become the precondition for future reinvestment and therefore gentrification. Such cycles cannot last forever, but for the last several decades, New York's planners and investors have managed to turn each near bust into another boom.

4
The Developer President and the Private Side of Planning History

Who is the landlord in the White House? How did his family's rise track with the history of US urban planning?

In January 2017, the United States took a giant leap toward real estate rule: Donald Trump, a man whose fortune stems largely from luxury property development, was inaugurated as the country's forty-fifth president.[1] In some ways this represented a return to form: the country's first president, George Washington, was also one of its largest landowners. But as an urban luxury developer, Trump's business model was decidedly more modern. With his election, it was now not just real estate in the aggregate that ruled, but an actual racist landlord running the country.

Trump's background as a developer is one of the most important factors in understanding the man and his mortally ludicrous presidency. While he may have been more famous as a reality

---

1   This account is heavily indebted to three books: Blair, Gwenda. *The Trumps: Three generations of builders and a presidential candidate*. Simon and Schuster, 2016 [2001]; Barrett, Wayne. *Trump: The deals and the downfall*. HarperCollins, 1992; Kranish, Michael and Marc Fisher. *Trump revealed: The definitive biography of the 45th president*. Scribner, 2016.

television host, celebrity endorser and prosperity proselytizer, he made his fortune buying, building, managing and licensing luxury apartments, clubs, casinos, office towers, hotels and golf courses, first in New York and then around the world. He is a product and an embodiment of real estate capital's global ascendency.

Trump's election cannot be explained by any one phenomenon. Economic decline, bigotry, misogyny, the failure of liberalism—all of these are important factors in explaining how this remarkable clod came to occupy one of the world's most powerful positions. But there is one line that can be drawn all the way through Donald Trump's career; in fact, this line extends all the way to his father, Fred, who passed on a tax-sheltered fortune to his son and jump-started his career; it can even be traced back to the president's father's father, Friedrich, a German immigrant and devoted hustler: through every rise, in every step toward power, the Trumps were enabled and encouraged by the changing winds of US urban planning. None of their achievements would have been possible without help from planners on the city, state and national scales. Each emerging pattern of planning created opportunities for successive generations of Trumps to grasp and hold on to, as private property, personal profit and generational wealth. The Trump family saga makes clear who, exactly, has benefited from the historical development of the real estate state, and just how they did it.

The Trumps were never quite leaders in their fields. There were always others who did what they did bigger and better (though never quite as loudly). Until recently, the Trumps were just a vulgar version of the completely normal capitalist developer. Their very ordinariness, however, is exactly what makes them a worthy case study. Taking a closer look at the Trumps allows us to see the flip side of planners' strategies in a private land market—the landowners who keep the public benefits that planners create, manage and distribute. In this sense, the Trumps are not just a real estate family, but emblems of the private side of US planning history.

Friedrich Trump: Profiting Off Proto-Planning

Friedrich Trump was born in 1869 in Kallstadt, a Bavarian wine-making village not yet incorporated into the German empire. At the age of sixteen, he fled conscription and immigrated to the United States. Sponsored by his older sister through an early version of "family reunification" immigration, Friedrich arrived in New York in 1885, the same year as the Statue of Liberty.[2]

If he had come from many other parts of the world, he would have been turned away. The Naturalization Act of 1870, the Page Act of 1875, the Chinese Exclusion Act of 1882, the Alien Contract Labor Law of 1885 and many other laws severely restricted workers from most countries seeking to enter the United States. Lawmakers classified Germans, however, as hardworking Whites, and largely encouraged their

---

2   Blair, *The Trumps*. Though Friedrich was commonly known as Fredrick or Fred in the US, I will continue to call him Friedrich in order to distinguish from his middle child, whom I will exclusively call Fred.

continued migration. Between 1820 and 1880, over three million Germans immigrated to the United States.[3]

Like many other German immigrants, Friedrich followed an established settlement pattern: first he lived on the Lower East Side of Manhattan; then what would become Murray Hill; then Harlem. For five years he was a barber, earning a modest living cutting other Germans' hair. This, however, is not how Friedrich Trump made his fortune.

Rumors were buzzing of opportunities out west: gold and silver to mine, cheap land to claim, new infrastructure, intentionally lax laws and tons of finance capital. American proto-planners were helping to complete a genocidal westward expansion, and Friedrich wanted a part of it. He boarded a series of trains and headed to Seattle.

There, he established what family biographer Gwenda Blair calls "the Trump MO: scope out the best location (it tended to be in the red-light district); open a business (in this case, restaurants, at times on land to which he had no legal right); and offer customers (mostly rootless newcomers who had yet to see their first nugget) some right-now comfort in the form of booze and easy access to women."[4] In other words, Friedrich made his fortune buying and building brothels. He chased the routes of finance and railways, and set up shop—in Blair's phrase—"mining the miners."[5] Friedrich never mined a single ore, laid a track of rail, or even put his money toward

3 Tichenor, Daniel J. *Dividing lines: The politics of immigration control in America.* Princeton University Press, 2002.

4 Blair, *The Trumps*, 1–2.

5 Ibid., 61.

financing those projects. Instead, he profited off state and bank investments in land and industry, and skimmed money off workers—both the miners he charged and the sex workers, cooks and bartenders he employed.

In 1891, with $600 from personal savings and family gifts, he bought his first brothel, the Dairy Restaurant. Two years later he sold it and, with extra money from his mother, bought forty acres a dozen miles outside Seattle. He purchased this land from the Northern Pacific Railway, which had received it from the federal government in lieu of cash payments for building the railway. The first plot of Trump-owned land in the United States was therefore part of a complex plan to extend the railways and develop the American empire.[6]

Friedrich moved to nearby Monte Cristo and spotted a parcel by the site of a future train depot. He staked a mining claim on it without any intention to dig.[7] Instead, he built a hotel, restaurant and brothel on that small patch of earth, even though he had no legal right to the land above ground. This kind of lax land use law was an early example of governing through informality, or the active process of looking the other way in order to enable a desired—if not quite legal—result.[8]

After a storm crushed his roof, Friedrich moved back to Seattle and opened a new brothel three blocks from the first. The place was so profitable he repaid his mortgage within a month. At the same time, however, Friedrich continued to play

---

6　Ibid., 41–46.

7　Ibid., 59–60.

8　Roy, Ananya. "Urban informality: Toward an epistemology of planning." *Journal of the American Planning Association* 71.2 (2005): 147–58.

around with land use laws. He bought several mining claims on untapped land he did not own, then flipped the claims for a profit without ever digging a single hole.[9] He did not even know if there was any metal to be mined; all he knew was that as long as the rails continued to be built and the desperate continued to flock, he could make easy money by commoditizing space plus time.

Soon a major storm would destroy the town. Just before it hit, though, Friedrich sold his business and took off for the Yukon. In Bennett, British Columbia, he set up his most profitable businesses: the New Arctic Restaurant and Hotel, which featured scales on which miners could weigh their gold dust as payment for sex and booze, and the White Horse, the first business new arrivals would see when they stepped off the train at Bennett. He stayed a while and made a mint, but when a reformist mayoral candidate seemed likely to win, Friedrich sold the business. Once again he got out just in time—shortly after he skipped town, the brothel was busted and the town foundered.[10] That was the end of Friedrich's Western period, but it was not the last time he would profit off land and property made profitable by planners.

Fortune in hand, he went to Germany, where he met and married Elizabeth Christ. They moved back to the United States and settled in the Bronx, where he worked as a barber and hotel manager. They hated it, though, and returned to Kaiser Wilhelm II's Germany in 1904. Friedrich tried to

---

9   Blair, *The Trumps*, 66, 70, 77.
10   Ibid., 85-93.

regain citizenship, claiming "We are loyal Germans and stand behind the high Kaiser and the mighty German Reich."[11] It didn't work. They were refused for his past draft dodging and deported back to the United States in 1905, while Elizabeth was pregnant with their son Fred. Friedrich went back to barbering, this time at 60 Wall Street—a block away from a building his grandson Donald would come to own many years later.[12]

Once again, however, Friedrich caught wind of a big investment opportunity, made possible by state planning and finance. Queens had recently been incorporated into the City of New York, along with the Bronx, Brooklyn and Staten Island. He saw the Bronx changing all around him, and he suspected that Queens—then largely rural—would catch up fast. The city was about to build the Queensboro Bridge, connecting the borough to Midtown Manhattan, and the Pennsylvania Railroad was building new rail lines.

In 1908, right before the bridge was completed, Friedrich and Elizabeth bought a two-story house in Woodhaven. Two years later they moved in to one half of the house and rented the other half out. Soon they bought another house and some vacant land nearby, and moved in while renting the first property.[13]

Between then and 1915, when the Interborough Rapid Transit Company opened the Queens subway, the borough's population grew by 40 percent and land values soared. Friedrich and Elizabeth capitalized off this urbanization and all the investments the city was making in the land—gridding

---

11   Ibid., 101.
12   Ibid., 110.
13   Ibid., 111–12.

streets, building pipes, enabling rail and generally making the land buildable—and bought fourteen properties and five vacant lots.[14]

In 1918, Friedrich died in the great flu pandemic that swept the country. Elizabeth and their son Fred, just fifteen years old, took over the properties and began building on the vacant lots. In 1927 they incorporated as Elizabeth Trump & Son, and Fred took the reins of the family's burgeoning family real estate business.

Fred Trump: The Rational Comprehensive Builder

After working construction in high school and studying engineering at the Pratt Institute, Fred Trump started developing properties in Queens. He began with single-family homes in Woodhaven, Queens Village and Hollis, always financing the next project with the sale of the last. The 1920s were booming times, both for Queens and the property racket in general, but it would all come crashing down in 1929. The Depression hit, and millions plunged into poverty, hunger and homelessness. Fred, however, did all right; he spent the next six years running a supermarket, and kept his eye out for new opportunities created by the crisis.

His first big break was the fall of the Lehrenkrauss Corporation in 1934, and the foreclosure of thousands of Queens homes. Lehrenkrauss had issued $26 million in mortgages for 40,000

---

14   Ibid., 111–15.

homes.[15] Due to fraud and debt, however, they were going out of business and auctioning off their properties. Through some clever self-inflation, Fred managed to place the winning bid on Lehrenkrauss's mortgage-servicing department, giving him a stream of income from debt-paying borrowers as well as an inside scoop on homes that were about to fall into foreclosure and could be purchased cheaply.[16] Fred was back in the real estate game, with a great deal more firepower than his one-by-one projects had previously afforded him.

At the same time, the Roosevelt administration was searching for ways to jump-start the economy, and looked to mass homeownership and construction as one key pathway out of the Depression. Congress passed the National Housing Act of 1934, which established the FHA and its system of government-backed private mortgages. Under this program, the federal government would act as a backstop for banks against creditors who defaulted. This was an enormous boon to potential homeowners, who suddenly had access to capital, as well as to banks, whose lending risk fell dramatically, and to builders, who now had an enormous new pool of financiers and clients. It was also the beginning of institutionalized redlining, a long-term process of divestment from integrated and Black neighborhoods and investment in segregated White housing.

This enticed Fred Trump. In 1936—nine years after being arrested at a Queens Ku Klux Klan rally—Fred got his first FHA

---

15   Barrett, *Trump*, 32.
16   Blair, *The Trumps*, 126–34.

contract to build a 450-home row house project in East Flatbush, Brooklyn.[17] The federal government provided about $750,000 dollars in mortgage insurance for what Trump described as an "exclusive development," which qualified him for even larger amounts of private loans.[18] Soon he expanded to other parts of Flatbush and Crown Heights, and by 1937 had built over 2,000 government-financed homes for aspiring middle class Whites.

In 1941, with the Second World War in the air, Fred expanded his operation to Brighton Beach and told potential investors, "In the event of war, I believe that the profit will be quicker and larger."[19] He was right. That year the federal government established the Office of Production Management (OPM). The OPM was mostly in the business of converting industrial sites to military production, but they also sponsored real estate projects in "defense housing areas." Because Brooklyn had a Navy yard, the entire borough counted as such an area, and the OPM paid Fred to build 700 homes in Bensonhurst.[20]

This opened an even bigger opportunity. Through Section 608 of the National Housing Act, which provided enormous subsidies to build apartment complexes for war workers, Fred extended the Trump family business to the mid-Atlantic and midwest. In Norfolk, Virginia, Fred built his first rental complex, with over 1,300 apartments. Later he bought and managed

---

17 Bump, Philip. "In 1927, Donald Trump's father was arrested after a Klan riot in Queens." *The Washington Post*, February 29, 2016.

18 Kranish and Fisher, *Trump revealed*, 29.

19 Ibid., 30.

20 Blair, *The Trumps*, 155–56.

the 500-unit Gregory Estates in Prince George's County and the 1,200-unit Swifton Village in Cincinnati.

In these places, Fred operated as a slumlord, denying basic services to his tenants. This sparked Norfolk's first documented rent strike, and a lawsuit alleging Fred's federally subsidized rentals suffered from "a lack of hot running water, sporadic or nonexistent air conditioning and elevator service, improper swimming facilities, and insect and rodent infestation."[21] He eventually showed up at Gregory Estates after years of tenant complaints and was swiftly arrested for running "a slum property," denied a license to operate in Maryland, and forced to promptly fix and sell the property.[22]

In addition to being a slumlord, Fred was also a segregationist. Just as the FHA intended, his properties were designed to prevent what the government called "inharmonious" (i.e. integrated) development.[23] In 1947, Fred built Shore Haven, a Bath Beach complex for White veterans composed of thirty-two six-story buildings with 1,344 apartments. It received $9 million in FHA-backed loans and would become Brooklyn's biggest private housing project. Soon after, with the help of both federal subsidies and mafia-connected contractors, he built the similarly segregated Beach Haven on Brighton Beach.[24] In 1950 leftist folk singer Woody Guthrie moved in and was deeply disturbed by Trump's racism. In an unfinished song, he ruminated:

---

21   Barrett, *Trump*, 78–79.
22   Ibid., 78.
23   Kranish and Fisher, *Trump revealed*, 53.
24   Blair, 171–72.

> I suppose that Old Man Trump knows just
> how much racial hate
> He stirred up in the bloodpot of human hearts
> When he drawed that color line
> Here at his Beach Haven family project
> Beach Haven ain't my home!
> No, I just can't pay this rent!
> My money's down the drain,
> And my soul is badly bent!
> Beach Haven is Trump's tower
> Where no black folks come to roam,
> No, no, Old Man Trump!
> Old Beach Haven ain't my home![25]

The Guthries left Old Man Trump's White Haven in 1952.

Two years later, federal investigators accused Fred and many other Section 608 developers of being "real estate profiteers," or making enormous profits off loopholes in the wartime housing laws.[26] Fred and other developers had realized that if their projects came up under budget or ahead of schedule, they could keep the extra subsidies they were paid and the higher rents they collected. This would allow them to pay out of their mortgage quicker and call their extra earnings capital gains, which were (and are) taxed at a much lower rate than income. Fred also figured out that the subsidies were based on the number of units they built, not the number of rooms. He would

---

25   Kaufman, Will. "Woody Guthrie and Fred Trump." *Woody Guthrie Annual* 2 (2016): 44–53.

26   Blair, *The Trumps*, 176.

therefore pack his buildings with studios and one-bedrooms, even though the subsidies were aimed to provide housing for veterans with families. He had to sit through some blistering hearings, but Fred prevailed without a charge. He was, however, blacklisted from future federal development and sued by his tenants.[27]

This hardly slowed him down. Fred went back to building mansions in Queens and purchased another Section 608 complex in Staten Island.[28] In 1963, he partnered with rational comprehensive city planners on a massive "urban renewal" project in Fort Greene, a largely African American and actively industrial area near Downtown Brooklyn. Along with three other private partners, Fred convinced the city to use Title I of the Federal Housing Act of 1949 to clear twenty acres for private hospital, university and residential development, including his University Towers. Against the protests of neighborhood residents and workers, the Brooklyn Civic Center urban renewal project razed twenty-three blocks, which had held 259 industrial and residential buildings, and 8,200 largely union jobs. At the time it was the largest condemnation in US history.

That same year, Fred embarked on the biggest project of his life: Trump Village in Coney Island. Using Title I yet again, he convinced the city to displace 900 working class families from the beach-adjacent land. Most of those households moved to fire-prone bungalows on the west side of Coney Island, which

---

27   Ibid., 199.
28   Ibid.

were never made for winter residence.[29] A good deal of the land Fred wanted was reserved for Abraham Kazan, head of the union-affiliated United Housing Foundation, which planned to build a vast limited-equity co-op complex. Through his Democratic Party patronage network, however, Fred managed to finagle not only half of Kazan's land, but a lucrative tax break as well.[30]

Trump Village was the first large-scale project to be completed under New York City's 1961 citywide rezoning, which encouraged intensive redevelopment and privately owned public spaces. With its seven twenty-three-story buildings and 3,800 apartments laid out as "towers in a park," or high-rise buildings surrounded by privately built green space at odd angles, Trump Village was exactly the kind of program the city wanted to see. It also secured $60 million in state FHA funds from New York's Mitchell-Lama subsidy program, which kept five of the buildings relatively affordable until 2007, when they were sold as market-rate apartments.[31] Fred made sure to work every possible angle and managed to overcharge New York State as well. This time he set up shell companies to own his construction equipment, then rented the tools to himself at inflated prices and billed the state.[32]

Between the 1920s and 1970s, Fred made a fortune as the private builder of government-subsidized segregated housing. By the mid-1970s, when Fred's fourth child, Donald, had

---

29 Denson, Charles. *Coney Island: Lost and found*. Elsevier, 2002.
30 Freeman, *Working class New York*, 292.
31 Barrett, *Trump*, 61.
32 Ibid., 64.

joined the business, a couple of facts had changed. First, in those early years of the neoliberal era, both local and national governments were fast exiting the business of directly subsidizing affordable housing construction, and moving instead toward a more complicated and less effective system of tax breaks and vouchers. Second, racial discrimination in housing was formally outlawed by the Fair Housing Act—Title 8 of the 1968 Civil Rights Act—which sought to punish landlords and realtors who enforced segregation and to stop the government from encouraging it through lending, land use and tax policies. Both subsidies and segregation, however, were the basis of the Trump family business, and US landlordism in general.

The Fair Housing Act immediately challenged Fred's business model. In 1969, a Black man named Haywood Cash tried to rent an apartment in Cincinnati's Swifton Village, but was told his income was too low and there no vacancies. Cash reported this to a local civil rights group called HOME, whose agents sent a White person to ask for an apartment. Though his income was the same as Cash's, Swifton management told the White tester there were plenty of apartments to choose from. When the tester revealed his ruse, management cursed him and threw him out. Cash then sued using the recently passed Fair Housing Act, and Fred settled quietly. Cash moved in victorious.[33]

In 1971 and 1972, under suspicion that the Trumps were systematically violating the Fair Housing Act, the Justice

33   Blair, *The Trumps*, 247.

Department sent several undercover testers to see how their agents responded to questions about vacancies in their New York properties. Over and over again, Black testers were quoted inflated prices and told there were no vacancies. Just like in Cincinnati, however, White testers were told there was plenty of room at reasonable rents. Out of all the buildings sampled, just one contained a large number of Black households—Patio Gardens, in the part of Flatbush now known as Prospect Lefferts Gardens. While that complex was 40 percent Black, every other building sampled was between 96.5 percent and 100 percent White. Black applicants were coded internally as "number nine," and their applications were placed in specially marked folders. With this evidence, the federal government filed *United States of America v. Fred C. Trump, Donald Trump and Trump Management, Inc.* in 1973.[34]

The Trumps fired back with bluster, but they knew they had no case. Donald refused to settle and instead hired Roy Cohn, the reactionary lawyer who had served as Joseph McCarthy's chief counsel. Cohn encouraged the Trumps to countersue the government for $100 million in damages. The suit was baseless, but it stalled the litigation process. In 1975 the Trumps settled and agreed to virtually everything the state wanted: they said they would advertise in Black newspapers, give the Urban League notice of vacancies and stop discriminating against welfare recipients. The Trumps did none of this, however, and three years later the Justice Department hauled them back into court for contempt.

---

34 Kranish and Fisher, *Trump revealed*, 55–56.

From that point on, Donald ran the family business. It was the late 1970s: the country was in a vicious recession and the city was emerging from a capital strike. Sensing these changing winds and indulging his own avarice, Donald followed the evolution of urban planning and public policy toward new heights of development, profitability and malevolence. With $1 million from his father in a tax-sheltered trust fund and, later, $40 million in inheritance, Donald would move the family business across the river to Manhattan and pursue a strategy of glaringly gauche luxury development.[35]

Donald Trump, Part 1: The Neoliberal Playboy

Donald's first big deal was far outside New York City, and it portended the coming financialization of housing generally and affordable housing particularly. In 1972, he sold the family's Cincinnati veteran's housing project, Swifton Village, to Prudent, an early iteration of a real estate investment trust (REIT). REITs, which only became commonplace in the 1990s, are giant pools of investment capital that buy properties and pay dividends to faraway shareholders, thus transforming property ownership from an individual investment into a financial product. In recent years, they have targeted subsidized and rent controlled housing developments for purchase and sought to close their rent gaps. Donald profited early off this trend.

---

35   Kessler, Glenn. "Trump's false claim he built his empire with a 'small loan' from his father." *Washington Post*, March 3, 2016; Swanson, Ana. "The myth and the reality of Donald Trump's business empire." *Washington Post*, February 29, 2016.

With the Swifton deal behind him, he moved on to a much more elaborate score—a deal that would occupy him for the next two decades. Like his grandfather Friedrich before him, Donald was obsessed with the value of land in relation to infrastructure. But whereas Friedrich got rich speculating on rising land values along future rail routes, Donald profited from cheap land near current train tracks.

Donald's eye was fixed on the Pennsylvania and New York railroads along Manhattan's West Side. These lines had been crucial to the island's early industrial development, but by the 1960s both the rails and the borough's industrial economy were declining. As part of this process, New York's planners, like those in many other cities, came to view their borderlands as ideal sites for highway construction and rolled out wide belts of asphalt around their shuttered waterfronts. In addition to cutting people off from the water, this created competition for already ailing railroad operators.

In 1968, struggling to survive amid automotive competition and declining industry, the Pennsylvania and New York railroads merged into the ill-fated Penn Central Transportation Company. As one of its first moves, the company sought to shed its less profitable assets, including its rail yards at West 60th Street and West 34th Street. Together, they formed the largest piece of available land in Manhattan.[36] By 1974 Donald saw possibilities for profit and he pounced, putting in a bid to turn them into commercial and residential real estate developments. Building, though, would require some friendly

---

36   Barrett, *Trump*, 102.

actions from planners—particularly public financing and a significant rezoning.

Donald's proposal met some resistance. John Zuccotti, chair of the City Planning Commission and later first deputy mayor, was amenable to residential development on the 60th Street yards but wanted to keep 34th Street industrial.[37] The Trumps, however, had a friend in the newly elected mayor, Abe Beame, who came out of the same Brooklyn Democratic Club as Fred. In a private meeting with Donald, Fred, Zuccotti and Penn Central's Ned Eichler, Beame proclaimed, "whatever my friends Fred and Donald want in this town, they get."[38]

Without Zuccotti's support, Beame could not make the changes Donald needed to do the deal. In the meantime, however, the mayor could make absolutely sure the yards were dead. In the mid-1970s, during a major oil crisis that caused many other cities to reinvest in rail, New York's West Side yards sat still. If the city had revived the yards during these years, it could have not only boosted New York manufacturers, but also cut back on the number of trucks that rolled through the city's highways and contributed to dramatic racial health disparities. Instead, for most of the 1970s, the yards lay fallow. Donald Trump did not singlehandedly kill New York City manufacturing—it was dying already, and people like the Rockefellers have considerably more blood on their hands. But a man who knew Trump's history deeper than most, investigative journalist Wayne Barrett, argued that "Trump's simultaneous hold on both

37   Ibid.
38   Blair, *The Trumps*, 259.

of the potential terminal sites for almost half a decade may have been a fatal blow to a manufacturing revival in New York."[39]

Mayor Beame successfully waited out Zuccotti, who stepped down in 1977. Shortly thereafter, in his final months in office, Beame approved Donald's plan (even though Donald had not yet bought all the land) and gave him an option to build. Soon thereafter Donald convinced the city to pay him $833,000 for permission to build a convention center on the 34th Street segment, further cementing the city's turn toward tourism over manufacturing.[40]

Trump then focused his sights on the Upper West Side yards. He finally bought that land—74.6 acres, plus 18.6 more underground—in 1986 and claimed he would build on it the world's tallest building. This did not exactly pan out, and over the next ten years the plan went through a multitude of mutations. By 1992, Donald had struck a deal with local politicians and resident associations to build "Trump Place," also known as "Riverside South," a slightly smaller but still expansive strip of luxury glass condominiums along the Hudson River. After twenty years assembling the capital, land, subsidies and zoning, he had finally won. Just a year and a half later, though—in a move recalling his grandfather Friedrich's mining claim speculation schemes—he sold the development rights to the Hong Kong-based New World Development Company for $88 million plus $250 million in debt repayment.[41] Donald

---

39   Barrett, *Trump*, 102.
40   Barro, Josh. "Donald Trump and the art of the public sector deal." *New York Times*, September 18, 2015.
41   Blair, *The Trumps*, 449.

had essentially played a very long con on the city, its planners, manufacturers, workers and community groups.

Along the way, Penn Central began shedding its Manhattan real estate holdings, which included an ailing hotel next to Grand Central Station. In 1975 Donald bought the Commodore Hotel with a plan to turn it into a shining glass high-rise known as the Grand Hyatt. The only way he could secure financing for the project, he claimed, was with a significant break on future property taxes. Given that 1975 was the year of the worst fiscal crisis in the city's history, then might not have been the best time to demand a tax cut—though he did go to the state legislature and try.[42]

Behind the scenes, however, Donald—with Fred's help— negotiated one of the largest and most galling commercial tax breaks ever seen in New York City. It signaled a distinct turn away from the uneven Keynesianism of rational comprehensive planning and toward the neoliberal model.

First, city and state planners had to call Trump's midtown hotel development an "industrial project" in order for it to be characterized as an economic development program. Then they had to declare the neighborhood—East 42nd Street and Park Avenue, just about the ritziest address in Manhattan—to be "blighted." The same terminology that rational comprehensive planners had earlier mobilized to justify "slum clearance" and "urban renewal" was now being used to validate corporate giveaways and luxury development.

---

42   Ibid., Barrett, *Trump*, 114.

Next, Trump would "sell" the land for $1 to the Urban Development Corporation (UDC). The UDC was the state's housing developer, created by Governor Nelson Rockefeller. The agency had the power to override local land use laws, building codes and tax arrangements in order to encourage housing construction. Over the years, however, the agency took on far more debt than it could repay and faced an existential crisis. Later in the 1970s, it would be restructured into an "economic development" agency and become one of the state's leading prison builders.[43] In 1975, though, it needed a reason to exist, and developers like Trump could provide it.

With the UDC technically in possession of the Grand Hyatt, the state would pay taxes to itself and lease the building to Trump for a small fee.[44] The size and longevity of that fee would be decided by Trump family ally Mayor Beame. In terms of longevity, Beame stretched the abatement for the longest period ever granted in New York at that time: forty years.[45] The fee's amount was linked to the building's profitability, but to ensure Donald's tab remained low, Beame had his people craft an unusually narrow definition of profits. For the purposes of this agreement, profit was defined as the "aggregate amount of monies actually received." The key words here are the last two. By pegging profit to "actually received" income, Donald was allowed to deduct any improvements he made to

---

43 Norton, Jack. "Little Siberia, star of the north: The political economy of prison dreams in the Adirondacks," in Morin, Karen M. and Dominique Moran (eds). *Historical geographies of prisons: Unlocking the usable carceral past.* Routledge, 2015, 168–84.

44 Blair, *The Trumps*, 285.

45 Freeman, *Working class New York*, 292.

the building, as well as any money spent on upkeep and maintenance. The tax break would be worth about twice as much as the standard abatement, for which this project would not even have qualified.[46] Simply creating a new tax break for Donald Trump, however, would be a little too blatant. Instead, the UDC created the "Business Incentive Program" to provide public subsidies to commercial developments. To no one's surprise, Trump's Grand Hyatt Hotel was the program's first recipient.[47]

The West Side yards and Grand Hyatt experiences taught Donald a great deal about the neoliberal planning environment in which he was operating. In the 1930s through the '60s, Fred figured out that the state was interested in subsidizing social reproduction for middle class Whites, and sought every opportunity to exploit that desire. In the 1970s and '80s, Donald realized that the austerity state was unlikely to hand out cash for ordinary housing construction, but would gladly suspend taxes and provide land and airspace for luxury development that would increase land values and rebrand the city.[48] He took these lessons and applied them to his Manhattan magnum, Trump Tower.

The building was constructed on the site of the former Bonwit Teller department store. To transform this stately store into a gigantic black box, Donald wanted two things: permission to build bigger than would otherwise be allowed, and an enormous tax break.

---

46   Barrett, *Trump*, 134.

47   Ibid., 119.

48   Greenberg, Miriam. *Branding New York: How a city in crisis was sold to the world*. Routledge, 2009.

Donald played a couple of tricks to ensure he would be granted the maximum zoning capacity. First, he produced horrendously ugly depictions of what the building would look like if it did not receive a rezoning and had to be built as of right. Next, he offered the Bonwit Teller Corporation a conditional lease that was premised on a larger floor size than the current zoning allowed. If the city wanted to keep Bonwit Teller in business and not end up with an architectural atrocity, it would have to give Donald his rezoning. The Planning Commission obliged, and the twelve-story building could suddenly be fifty-eight stories.[49]

Donald also availed himself of a lucrative "density bonus" written into the 1961 citywide rezoning—a privately owned public space. By putting a "public atrium" in the entryway and two interior gardens on upper floors, Trump Tower was allowed to rise an additional twenty stories worth an estimated $530 million.[50]

With his rezoning and bonus in hand, Donald set out to grab as large a tax break as possible. In 1983 he applied for 421-a, the state's grandest geobribe, but was denied by the city's department of Housing Preservation and Development (HPD). Undeterred, Donald sued the city and won a $20 million break on his tax bill.[51] Not only did he get to keep his money, Donald also recruited the HPD commissioner, Anthony Gliedman, to

49   Barrett, *Trump*, 172–73.

50   Elstein, Aaron. "Trump Tower fined over missing bench after the presumptive GOP nominee skips hearing." *Crain's New York Business*, June 23, 2016.

51   Gaiter, Dorothy J. "City ordered to give abatement on taxes to the Trump Tower." *New York Times*, June 19, 1983.

leave city government and become one of his many political fixers.[52] Years later, in 2004, Donald would secure an additional twenty-year "Industrial and Commercial Abatement" for the building from the city's public-private Economic Development Corporation worth an astounding $163.775 million.[53]

Trump Tower cost Donald roughly $200 million to build, but the initial condominium sales alone brought in $277 million. Since then, he has reaped tremendous profits, all the while paying precious little in property taxes.

At the same time, Donald secured the 421-a tax abatement for Trump Plaza on the Upper East Side. His argument was perfectly pitched to neoliberal planners. Like every other developer, he claimed his ultra-luxury co-op deserved a tax break because it would create jobs and attract wealthy outsiders and corporations to the city. Donald went a step further than most, though, and claimed the city should lower his tax bill because his building would raise neighborhood prices, thus displacing middle class Manhattanites and sending them out to gentrify the outer boroughs.[54] His $13 million tax break was approved.[55]

Around this time, Trump set his sights on a lifetime goal: owning and operating a luxury casino. Since most types of gambling were illegal in New York City and its suburbs, he turned to New Jersey's Atlantic City. In the 1980s, the city was in rough shape and desperate for some sort of economic

---

52 Frieden and Sagalyn, *Downtown, inc.*, 226.
53 Melchior, Jillian Kay. "Donald Trump has mastered the art of the tax break." *National Review*, August 19, 2015.
54 Blair, *The Trumps*, 327.
55 Bagli, Charles V. "A Trump empire built on inside connections and $885 million in tax breaks." *New York Times*, September 17, 2016.

turnaround. Into this void Donald appeared, hawking a vision of luxury casinos for the hardscrabble city. He offered the same sort of corporate-led tourism gentrification that was transforming places like New York's Times Square and New Orleans' French Quarter. Just like in Manhattan, Donald had two requests: public financing and land use leeway. Atlantic City gave him both.

To finance the project, the city floated its first privately placed bond issue—or a bond targeted toward a small number of very large investors, in this case from Bear Stearns—and its first bond for a private corporation's project. The way the bond was structured, neither Donald nor the Trump Organization were on the hook; it was backed by the full faith and credit of the city. In other words, if Trump's casino failed, the largely poor residents of Atlantic City would have to pay for it with their meager tax revenues. This $353 million bond provided Donald with 100 percent of the financing he needed, plus an extra $5 million "fee."[56]

Gambling is a highly regulated industry, and building an Atlantic City casino would require extensive interventions from state regulators and planners. Donald's casino review, however, was the fastest in the state's history. He leveraged one of the primary characteristics of neoliberal urbanism toward his own purposes: a race-to-the-bottom competition between cities for mobile capital, foreshadowing more recent interurban scrambles for corporate investment like the debased contest for Amazon's second corporate headquarters. Atlantic City

---

56   Blair, *The Trumps*, 350.

was terrified of casino competition, so they tried to secure developers like Donald who might prefer to build in New York but at the time could not. In exchange for lucrative geobribes, developers would lobby against casino expansion in New York because it would compete with their New Jersey investments.[57] Between competing cities, the developers won.

In this case, Atlantic City planners gave Donald all sorts of favorable conditions and approved just about every absurd demand he made. In one small but telling example, Donald demanded that he be permitted to build bridges between his casino towers, allowing customers to travel from one build-ing to another without setting foot on the city's streets. This would not only interfere with ocean views—one of Atlantic City's selling points—but, more importantly, keep people from walking through the city and spending their money outside of Trump's developments, which was a central premise of the city's economic development strategy. Nonetheless, Donald got his skyways.[58]

Once in operation, Atlantic City planners continued their laissez-faire approach, even as Trump's behavior grew increas-ingly erratic and his finances became untenable. Rather than take enforcement action, they looked the other way out of fear that they might put him out of business.[59]

Meanwhile, back in Manhattan, Donald was stepping up his privatization game. Not content seeking giveaways from the state, he now wanted to run parts of it for profit. His first

57   Barrett, *Trump*, 215.
58   Ibid., 231.
59   Blair, *The Trumps*, 343.

target was the Central Park skating rink—a small but lucrative mark, and a way of needling an adversary, Mayor Koch.

The rink had been closed from 1980 to 1986, following a disastrous (if well-intentioned) experiment in alternative energy. The ice would not freeze, causing a major headache for Mayor Koch, who finally went to the Board of Estimate with a plan to fix it. Still stinging from the Koch administration's initial denial of his Trump Tower tax abatement, Donald jumped at the opportunity to humiliate the mayor. According to Koch political biographer Jonathan Soffer, "A keen neo-liberal, [Donald Trump] also saw a way to communicate an ideological message, that the private sector was more efficient than government, and offered to take charge of rebuilding the rink."[60]

Once again leaning on his father's political connections, he convinced the board to deny Koch's plan and instead fund his company to do virtually the same thing, in the same time frame and for the same amount of money. Garnering favors from contractors who wanted to work on future Trump projects and benefiting from the oversight of former Koch administration member Gliedman, Trump completed the renovation in just five months. His successful political cronyism became a case study in free-market triumphalism; in historian Joshua Freeman's telling, "the media hailed him as the embodiment of one of the lessons of the fiscal crisis: let the genius of private enterprise replace the morass of government bureaucracy."[61]

---

60   Soffer, Jonathan. *Ed Koch and the rebuilding of New York City*. Columbia University Press, 2010, 262.

61   Freeman, *Working class New York*, 292.

The rink now operates as a private concession within the park and contributes to the Trumps' wealth.

This phase of Donald's career, covering roughly the 1970s through the early 1990s, was characterized by schemes to privatize public land, secure generous land use exemptions, leverage public financing for private development and profit off the city's deindustrialization. As city planning turned neoliberal, Donald turned a mighty profit. But in the late 1980s and early 1990s, a moment when Donald was holding on to an enormous amount of debt, the country faced a recession and he flew into a tailspin. Property values were dropping and some scholars were wondering if this was the end of gentrification. It was not, but it was the end of Donald's career as a straightforward developer.

While others went out of business, Trump turned out all right. According to biographer Gwenda Blair, his creditors considered him "too big to fail" and mostly renegotiated their interest rates instead of foreclosing on his properties.[62] He used the corporate bankruptcy laws to his favor and mutated into a different kind of capitalist.

Donald Trump, Part 2: The Deregulated Swindler

In the late 1990s and 2000s, Donald shifted from building to branding. He sold his surname to other people's projects, including developments around the United States as well as in Argentina, Azerbaijan, Bermuda, Brazil, Canada, the Dominican

---

62   Blair, *The Trumps*, 6.

Republic, Dubai, Egypt, Germany, Georgia, the Grenadines, India, Indonesia, Ireland, Israel, Mexico, Panama, the Philippines, Qatar, Saint Martin, Saint Vincent, Saudi Arabia, South Korea, Turkey, United Arab Emirates, the United Kingdom and Uruguay. In addition to real estate, he specialized in industries that were undergoing substantial deregulation, from airlines (Trump Shuttle) to for-profit colleges (Trump University) to Ponzi-like "multilevel marketing" schemes (Trump Network).[63] For Donald, the beauty of these deals was that even though nearly all of them failed and stripped countless individuals of their assets, he always walked away with a profit.[64]

During this period, the biggest deregulated market was in home mortgages. The industry for securitized subprime—or awful mortgages sold in pieces to multiple parties around the world—was made possible by two major deregulations, one passed by Reagan and the other by Clinton.

In the 1980s, the Reagan administration worked closely with Lewis Ranieri of Salomon Brothers to slash federal regulations on the home loan industry, and to legitimize and popularize securitization as a strategy to minimize individual lenders' risk. Two decades later, it was one of the driving features of the global finance sector, with investment banks, hedge funds, insurance companies and pension funds owning small pieces of millions of home loans through mortgage-backed securities, collateralized debt obligations and other financial derivatives. In sociologist Kevin Fox Gotham's terms, securitization was

---

63　Kranish and Fisher, *Trump revealed*, 221–39.
64　Ibid., 224.

about "creating liquidity out of spatial fixity," or turning the very geographic specificity of land and homeownership into a flexible financial tool.[65]

In 1999, the Clinton administration pushed Congress to repeal the Glass-Steagall Act, a Depression-era law that abolished the antagonism between commercial and investment banking. This allowed securitized subprime to become big business for banks at all levels and incentivized them to shift their investment priorities toward the ballooning real estate market. All this building and investment was also encouraged by historically low interest rates, kept down by Federal Reserve chairman Alan Greenspan despite many signs of a looming crisis.

By the middle of the aughts, a terrifyingly high portion of the global economy—roughly 70 percent of financial transactions—was caught up in this web, and it was all based on punitive home mortgages.[66] This was a disturbing enterprise for many reasons. Most simply, it was a way of making huge amounts of money off a system that was sure to dispossess millions of people. It was also an economy feeding on itself; as the market for mortgage-backed securities and their myriad derivatives grew, the housing market boomed. Home values shot to unsustainably high rates as wages stagnated, inducing low- and moderate-income mortgagers to take on more debt at less favorable rates.

---

65   Gotham, Kevin Fox. "Creating liquidity out of spatial fixity: The secondary circuit of capital and the subprime mortgage crisis." *International Journal of Urban and Regional Research* 33.2 (2009): 355–71.

66   Sassen, Saskia. "Expanding the terrain for global capital." In Aalbers, Manuel B. (ed.). *Subprime cities: The political economy of mortgage markets.* Wiley-Blackwell, 2012: 74–96.

In 1936, Fred Trump saw possibilities for profit in the federal government's entrance into the home mortgage market. In 2006, Donald saw opportunity in the federal government's mortgage deregulation.

Trump Mortgage was a brokerage company, acting as a middleman between borrowers and lenders. The idea came from his first child, Donald Jr, but it was the elder Donald who was listed as a partner, along with a banker named E.J. Ridings. The company brokered residential and commercial real estate loans in fifteen states, promising fast approvals and leaning heavily on the Trump aesthetic. Its website was filled with images of glitzy Trump properties and its phone number was 888-79-TRUMP. The staff consisted of the sleaziest sellers available, many of whom had been fired from other mortgage companies.[67]

Their office in Trump's 40 Wall Street tower was divided into two sections. In one part of the office, sales associates matched wealthy contacts with mortgages for high-end residential and commercial properties. On the other side was their "boiler room," stuffed with brokers cold-calling working class people and trying to convince them to either buy a property with a subprime mortgage or refinance their home at dubious rates.[68] Between the two, the company brokered $1 billion in predatory mortgages.[69]

---

67   Fredrickson, Tom. "Undoing of Trump Mortgage." *Crain's New York Business*, August 5, 2007.

68   Kranish and Fisher, *Trump revealed*, 235.

69   Hamburger, Tom and Michael Kranish. "Trump Mortgage failed. Here's what that says about the GOP front runner." *Washington Post*, February 29, 2016.

Though Donald had already made money off the naming rights, the company did not last long. A lot went wrong: it started just two months after the peak of subprime sales; its chief executive, Ridings, was fired for fabricating most of his resume; several of the top managers left quickly; and the company only did about a third of the business it projected for its first year. After just eighteen months, Trump Mortgage closed. Donald blamed its failure on others and, after the company stopped paying rent, he successfully sued himself for eviction.[70] He sold the company and the naming rights to First Meridian Mortgage, which ran it as Trump Financial for a couple of years before folding.[71]

In his own small way, Donald contributed directly to the subprime boom and bust. What he was saying about the mortgage crisis, however, is just as revealing as what he did to stoke it. While promoting Trump Mortgages, he was completely bullish on the subprime market. In 2006, when he was first launching the company, he told CNBC, "I think it's a great time to start a mortgage company" and "the real estate market is going to be very strong for a long time to come."[72] A few months later, he claimed, "Trump Mortgage is going to take better care of people than anyone in the mortgage industry ever has."[73]

That same year, however, he was telling prospective Trump University customers that he was rooting for the housing

70   Simones, Ivylise. "The Trump files: In which Donald sues himself— and wins! (And loses.)" *Mother Jones*, October 5, 2016.

71   McKnight, Jenna M. "Trump mortgage—take two." *The Real Deal*, September 15, 2007.

72   Hamburger and Kranish, "Trump Mortgage failed."

73   Simones, "The Trump files."

bubble to burst. "I sort of hope that happens because then people like me would go in and buy. People like me would go in and buy like crazy."[74] By 2008 he was running Trump University advertisements in newspapers around the country claiming he could teach customers how to exploit their neighbors' misfortune. The text of one ad read, "Investors Nationwide are Making Millions in Foreclosures ... AND SO CAN YOU!"[75] In another, Donald was more explicit. The ad read:

Foreclosures rose 94% in 2007, and I am confident they will keep rising. This high-volume trend means you won't be searching for available deals. You just need to know where to look for the best ones.

The current rise in foreclosures is an incredible opportunity for you to make legendary real estate deals. It's time to achieve the privileged life you've always dreamed about ... not years from now, but just a few short months from now. Investing in foreclosures could make you a millionaire by this time next year.[76]

As people lost their homes to the kinds of predatory loans Trump Mortgages brokered, Donald was preaching the prosperity gospel of accumulation by dispossession. He thus

74   Diamond, Jeremy. "Donald Trump in 2006: I 'sort of hope' real estate market tanks." *CNN*, May 19, 2016.
75   Ellipses in the original. Laughland, Oliver and Mae Ryan. "'Donald Trump was part of the problem.' Cleveland's subprime lesson for Republicans." *The Guardian*, July 16, 2016.
76   Ellipses in the original; Kaczynski, Andrew. "Become a millionaire in a year, Trump promised in an ad for Trump University." *Buzzfeed*, March 14, 2016.

managed to make money off both selling bad mortgages and teaching others how to profit from the immiseration those mortgages inevitably produced. It was all made possible by a planning and regulatory system that decided to leave mortgages to the market and encourage speculation, securitization and, ultimately, pauperization. By the end of the crisis, 13 million US households would face foreclosure, and Donald Trump would come out on top.[77]

Donald Trump, Part 3: President of the Real Estate State

Eight years and countless outrages later, Donald Trump became the United States' first developer president. His agenda is far reaching—terrorizing migrants, banning Muslims, slashing regulations, reducing social programs and expanding the military—but improving real estate futures is never far from the president's mind. The day before his inauguration, Trump's notorious legal fixer Michael Cohen told an industry paper Trump would be a boon to real estate, particularly in New York City. Without spelling out the details, he stated, "There's going to be a lot of money in the hands of a lot of people. When that happens, you'll see a lot more home purchasing and a lot more construction, which is not only good for developers but for everyone."[78]

The clearest expression of Trump's presidential real estate agenda was his initial set of appointments. His choice for HUD

---

77   Sassen, Saskia. *Expulsions*. Harvard University Press, 2014, 219.
78   Branzel, Kathryn and Will Parker. "America gets its first developer-in-chief." *The Real Deal*, January 20, 2017.

secretary, Ben Carson, had no experience managing public housing, distributing housing subsidies or challenging housing discrimination. In fact, his most famous contribution to housing policy debates was a full-throated denunciation of public intervention into the real estate market. In 2015, after the Obama administration created new HUD rules to encourage incremental integration, Carson called fair housing laws—the very statutes used to prosecute Fred and Donald for discrimination in the 1970s—an example of "the history of failed socialist experiments in this country."[79]

This made Carson a leading candidate for the job of enforcing the Fair Housing Act—along with avid racist Jeff Sessions, now attorney general. According to Seema Agnani of the National Coalition for Asian Pacific American Community Development, opposing fair housing was Carson's "central qualification for the job. It is license for racist landlords to discriminate more openly, for racist city leaders to more aggressively create policies and allocate resources in ways that segregate and exploit communities of color. It is the signal of the intent to dismantle fair housing as we know it."[80]

Under Trump and Carson's watch, HUD's already emaciated budget could be further starved, with public housing taking the biggest hit. At the time of this writing, Congress has not actually approved a budget, opting instead to sidestep the process and issue a string of "continuing resolutions" that have

79   Carson, Ben S. "Experimenting with failed socialism again." *Washington Times*, July 23, 2015.
80   Agnani, Seema. "The president as developer-in-chief." *Rooflines*, January 13, 2017.

not yet targeted HUD. Nonetheless, the president has issued budget proposals, which set out his (or his staff's) preferred spending priorities. Trump's first proposed budget would have withheld $7.4 billion from HUD, representing a 15 percent cut. Trump and Carson have also introduced legislation that would simultaneously increase rents and deny repairs for public and subsidized housing residents, add work requirements to several housing programs, terminate vouchers for a quarter million low-income households, cut Homeless Assistance grants, and eliminate both Community Development Block Grants and the National Housing Trust Fund, which provide federal support for low-income housing development. If successful, such changes would recall HUD's punitive approach to post-Katrina New Orleans, which Clyde Woods characterized as "impoverishment, asset stripping, and racial enclosure policies," and generalize it throughout the country.[81]

To lead the Treasury Department—the agency responsible for managing the post-mortgage crisis bank bailout, among other things—Trump chose Steven Mnuchin, a Goldman Sachs alum and hedge fund manager. Between 1994 and 1999, before being promoted to executive vice president, Mnuchin helped Goldman develop their mortgage securitization program, which would become a prime driver of the housing crisis and rob millions of their homes and savings.[82] After the crash, Mnuchen's hedge fund bought one of the country's most

---

81   Woods, Clyde. "Les miserables of New Orleans: Trap economics and the asset stripping blues, Part 1." *American Quarterly* 61.3 (2009): 769–96, 770.
82   Immergluck, Dan. "The foreclosure king ascends to treasury." *Rooflines*, December 7, 2016.

predatory lenders, IndyMac, and ran it as OneWest. OneWest continued aggressively foreclosing on indebted mortgagees, earning Mnuchin the moniker "foreclosure king" among California housing activists.[83] All this made Mnuchin a perfect choice for Treasury secretary under Trump, where he will not only manage the nation's finances, but also oversee the Low-Income Housing Tax Credit (the primary vehicle for financing new affordable housing construction) and the Treasury's Geographic Targeting Order (which scrutinizes large cash real estate purchases made under fake names in Manhattan and Miami).

Trump's senior advisor is his son in law, Jared Kushner. Kushner is a player in the northeast and mid-Atlantic real estate scenes, with residential and commercial projects in Manhattan, Brooklyn, Jersey City, Philadelphia, Pittsburgh, Baltimore and beyond. Mayor de Blasio has stated publicly of Jared Kushner, "I respect him a lot. He's someone who really cares about New York City and is someone that would be very helpful to us." Kushner's renters, however, were horrified at the prospect of their landlord in the White House. One of the rent-stabilized tenants he spent years harassing told a reporter, "Trump's appointment of Kushner is in keeping with his cabinet selections of amoral billionaire crooks, liars, and thieves … The whole country's going to experience what we've been going through."[84]

83 Levin, Sam. "Inside Trump treasury nominee's past life as 'foreclosure king' of California." *The Guardian*, December 2, 2016.

84 Wishnia, Steven. "Jared Kushner's East Village tenants 'horrified' their landlord will be working in the White House." *The Village Voice*, January 12, 2017.

While planning is largely a local government function, President Trump has enormous power over its contours. His taxing and spending decisions greatly determine the funds local governments have to work with. Trump's tax cuts, his one major legislative accomplishment in his first two years in office, not only limited the amount of money available to cities but acted as a superfluous stimulus to the commercial real estate industry: while some homeowners in higher-tax states saw their taxes mount, landlords and investors—particularly those involved in REITs—reaped benefits. His regulators will make decisions about what practices to allow (more development everywhere) and what to deny (any challenge to exploitive real estate practices). The infrastructure projects he green-lights—which were originally coordinated by fellow New York City real estate developers Stephen Ross and Richard LeFrak—will not only provide investors with permanent revenue streams through tolls and other fees, but will enrich nearby landowners.

As president, Trump not only has the power to make himself and his family even wealthier, but to further enrich the entire class of transnational real estate capitalists and advance the project of real estate rule. This is certainly evident in his domestic agenda, but even his foreign policy seems inflected by the abiding class consciousness of a landlord and developer. In his first press conference after meeting with North Korea's Kim Jong-un, Trump named hotel and condo development as a potential positive outcome of political reform:

They have great beaches. You see that whenever they're exploding their cannons into the ocean. I said, "Boy, look at that view. Wouldn't that make a great condo?" You could have the best hotels in the world right there. Think of it from a real estate perspective. You have South Korea, you have China and they own the land in the middle. How bad is that, right? It's great.[85]

Never has real estate capital been more powerful, at every scale of US government. Until recently, the Trumps were bit players in that transition, but their story is indicative of the transformation. As real estate rose in centrality to urban and national politics, developers, investors and schemers like the Trumps made enormous profits off cities' development and eventual gentrification. The Trump family saga shows the progression of real estate in relation to planning over time: first from opportunists (like Friedrich) who capitalized on planners' work; then to builders (like Fred) who were directly financed by the state; and finally to tycoons (like Donald) who starved the state before seizing it. Like the larger class of real estate developers, the Trumps played planners for profit and walked away with the country.

---

85   New York Times staff. "6 highlights from Trump's news conference." *New York Times*, June 12, 2018.

5
Unmaking the Real Estate State

What more can we imagine?
What is to be done?

A great deal of urban politics comes down to who owns the city. Land and building owners have long held outsized power, but the onslaught of gentrification and the rise of the FIRE economy has strengthened their grip over urban life. While developer-kings like Trump have driven this transformation and benefited most from it, urban planners are profoundly implicated in developing the spatial strategies that turn cities into luxury products. The real estate state, however, is a historical and political construct: it was formed by historical factors, and it can be unmade by political movements.

Given the serious structural constraints on planning in capitalist cities, it is hard to imagine planners taking a serious stand against gentrification. Yet there are many planners, both inside and outside government, who seek to do just that.

The planning profession can appeal to liberal technocrats and conservative incrementalists, but it still continues to draw radicals into its ranks. Social democrats become planners in the hopes of expanding the welfare state. Socialists join the profession to develop public alternatives to private systems. Communists are attracted to the idea of comprehensive planning over markets. A surprising number of anarchists work as city planners, reflecting both the roots of western planning in anarchist geography and a common interest in punk transportation subcultures (like skateboarding and Critical Mass). There are radicals in planning departments throughout the country and around the world, and while they are tasked with raising property values and promoting gentrification, they have a deep desire to do otherwise. Just how to do so, however, remains elusive.

Observing Latin America's "pink tide," anthropologist Fernando Coronil commented, "the left has no map, but it has a compass."[1] Its participants may have lacked a complete vision, but they had a sense of which way to turn. This is true too in the case of US urban planning, where there is little agreement among radicals about the precise nature of "the good city" but there is a strong sense of what is wrong today: planning is too entwined with real estate; gentrification is displacing current residents, precluding future migrants and killing the city's core; and commoditized land markets are turning public improvements into private profits.

There is no silver bullet that will unmake the real estate state—no single planning tool, policy or law, no clever theoretical formation or historical precedent. There is, however,

---

1 Coronil, Fernando. "The future in question: History and utopia in Latin America (1989–2010)." In Calhoun, Craig J. and Georgi M. Derluguian (eds). *Business as usual: The roots of the global financial meltdown.* NYU Press, 2011, 260.

a great deal that can be done right now to reverse these trends and even more that can be dreamt for the future. Urban social movements—that is, not just political groupings that form in cities but movements focused around popular control over the shape and dynamics of urban space—can take the lead in diagnosing the problems with capitalist city planning, organizing for immediate state action to address them and imagining alternatives for a liberated society. Plans can change; planners can change; planning can change; but nothing will change simply because it ought to. Things will only change when people make them—people organized in buildings, neighborhoods and cities, through institutional and contentious politics, as a social force that can alter the balance of class power.

The particular form such movements will take is impossible to know and would be arrogant to diagnose. But as we're organizing and debating organizational form and strategy, we need to articulate not just what we are against, but what we are fighting for. In order to map these possibilities, I interviewed radicals within the New York City planning apparatus who daily face the conflict between planning's promise and its execution, and compared what I heard from them to the ideas emerging from the housing and planning movements in which I am situated.

Although it can be challenging to see beyond the limitations of our current system, everyone I spoke with agreed that something had to give. One hundred years from now, our cities will be unimaginably different. That change will come is certain. The form it takes, however, is up for grabs.

Policies

Given the power of the real estate industry and hostility of the federal government, few city administrations are taking bold leaps to challenge the status quo. This does not mean, however, that there is simply nothing to be done. Even within the current modes of republican government and capitalist production, there are policies that could address some of the problems of planning in the real estate state.

Planners are often admonished to build on what exists rather than dream up whole new systems and spaces. While this can be limiting and reproduce historical and structural inequalities, it's not always bad advice. There are some current policies that, if altered in important ways, would produce dramatically different results.

Take inclusionary zoning, a classic neoliberal policy—it leans on the private sector (developers) to produce a social good (affordable housing), and it does so by granting developers the ability to build bigger and therefore collect more rent. Applying the policy differently would not make it anything other than neoliberal, but if inclusionary zoning were *only* used in rich White enclaves and *never* in neighborhoods at risk of gentrification, its results would be notably different: forcing the wealthy to integrate at least a little bit, rather than gentrifying the city and calling it progress.

In New York City, inclusionary upzonings have almost exclusively targeted working class neighborhoods. During Mayor de Blasio's first term, the only rich neighborhood to be upzoned was Midtown East, and that action did not trigger inclusionary zoning because it applied only to commercial buildings. An analysis by planning advocate Moses Gates, however, shows that there are plenty of predominantly White, wealthy, low-density and transit-rich neighborhoods that could receive this treatment instead, including the most exclusive parts of Murray Hill, Bay Ridge and Forest Hills.[2] Altering its targeting would not make inclusionary zoning an ideal housing policy, but that crucial change—which would likely be fiercely contested by homeowners—would begin to alter the dynamics of development and displacement.

As we take the neoliberal strategies imposed on poor neighborhoods and force them instead on the rich, we can also demand the opposite: take the privileges embedded in rich places' plans and redistribute them. Fancy neighborhoods are the way they are not only because they have the money to sustain their buildings and businesses, but also because planners provide them with extra protections rarely afforded to their poorer neighbors. You cannot build a cheap apartment building in most wealthy low-rise zones, but you can build luxury condos in the places where most poor people live.

New York City's "special planned community preservation districts," for example, protect middle class enclaves (such as Queens' Sunnyside Gardens and Fresh Meadows), but just one particularly well-designed public housing project (Manhattan's Harlem River Houses). In these districts, any demolition

---

2   Gates, Moses. "To prevent worsening inequality, put affluent neighborhoods on NYC re-zoning list." *Metropolitics*, November 17, 2015.

or construction must go through a public approval process and obtain a special permit. This allows future generations to enjoy the built environment as it was planned, without having to fight off developers who want to capitalize on its original beauty. Nearly all the city's public housing, as well as many of its subsidized housing developments (like the 40,000 co-op apartments that unions built during the mid-twentieth century), fit the criteria for these preservation districts—they were built as planned units, with buildings and open spaces placed in careful calculation—yet only one receives this protection. Existing preservation tools could be expanded to protect working class environments from encroaching predatory development, preserve the class character of public and subsidized housing and ensure that any future development not only matches a planned community's aesthetic patterns but also its income mixes.

Planners can also find inspiration in the important victories that working class communities have secured during eras when real estate's grip was weaker. These grooves carved into the state's institutional materiality protect particular places from gentrification's most rapacious aspects and can be expanded to cover more ground.

In New York, rent regulations offer one of the strongest examples, though the laws' state control makes them difficult for city planners to influence. These laws are the product of early twentieth-century class conflict: rent strikes that swept Harlem, the Lower East Side and beyond, and created a crisis for landlords and the state. Rent regulation also had some support from the city's industrial capitalists, who saw rising housing prices as a source of pressure on wages. The rent laws are still in place for older buildings in certain counties, but over the years they have been chipped away many times: first the laws were taken over by the state, which is even less responsive to tenants than the city; then a series of loopholes were introduced that would allow for more frequent and severe rent increases; finally, a mechanism was created to allow landlords to withdraw apartments from the system after they reached a certain rent threshold and became vacant. Strengthening rent controls—eliminating the loopholes and making the protections permanent and universal—would be one of the most important ways to halt housing inflation and cut the cord that so clearly connects planning to gentrification. Donna Mossman of Brooklyn's Crown Heights Tenants Union frames her group's struggle to preserve and expand rent regulation as, in part, a way for people at risk of displacement to claim the benefits of public investment: "That's what we're fighting for. They're beautifying the neighborhood. I've been here for 36 years. I want to enjoy that also."[3]

In a few places, working class residents have bound together to form nonspeculative urban housing models in the center of otherwise overheated land markets. In New York's Cooper Square district, residents fought for fifty years against urban renewal and gentrification, and managed to secure the city's first community land trust. This complex form of land and property tenure, which originated among southern Black agricultural workers during the civil rights movement, operates

3   Marsh, Ian. "Tenants form union to fight gentrification." *City Limits*, March 3, 2014.

differently in different places, but the key elements are: the land is owned by one not-for-profit entity, including but not limited to the residents of buildings above; the buildings are owned cooperatively by the residents themselves; and long-term contracts restrict the sale of either the land, the buildings or the apartments for much more than the original owners paid. In many cases, resale is restricted to households with equivalent or lower incomes than the original buyer. When done right, the result is functionally decommodified land and housing. Cooper Square is still private—the apartments can be sold, and the government does not own it—but residents are no longer subject to the fluctuations of market speculation. While the New York State government has begun to dedicate a marginal amount of resources to community land trust development, it will take strong and sustained organizing to get access to the funding necessary to keep buildings deeply affordable to working class residents.

We should view these kinds of victories not as anachronisms or anatopisms, but rather as the basis for generalized protections. That would mean changing the default actions for city agencies from their current objectives of raising property values and selling off land and buildings to another program altogether: disincentivizing evictions and decommodifying land. It should be city policy to protect tenants' "right to stay put" over landlords' right to extract rents; what's more, whenever the city takes possession of land and property, it should maintain its public use.[4]

---

4   Hartman, "The right to stay put."

To beef up the stock of such land and properties, cities can adopt policies that facilitate the transfer of private land to the public. When property owners fail to pay taxes, cities can stop selling liens to speculators, as New York City currently does, and instead transfer tax-deficient properties into a scatter-site community land trust. Cities could pass "right to sell" bills, giving households at risk of foreclosure the opportunity to sell their home to the city, which would operate it as public housing. Cities could also institute a "right of first refusal" on home sales, as is being established in parts of Paris. Under this system, the city has a first pass at any property for sale, and can pay the seller market value for their home and convert it into social housing. Thanks to a ballot referendum, San Francisco's Small Sites Program has started buying out rent-controlled buildings and transferring ownership from private landlords to community land trusts.

While the idea of public buyouts may sound farfetched, it is a practice the federal government already engages in for less socially beneficial purposes. Under the Maiden Lane program, for example, the Federal Reserve purchased thousands of failing mortgages as part of its bank bailout. This was a massive, state-planned transfer of wealth to financial institutions. In the hands of tenants, however, the tool could be restructured as a way of decommodifying land and property in both gentrified and disinvested areas.

More plainly, city, state and federal governments can get back in the business of funding, acquiring and building public housing. After all, these programs are not failing on the basis of some inherent deficiency in the policy; they are faltering because they are chronically starved of financial resources and the federal government refuses to fund further expansions. There is, of course, plenty of money in the federal budget, with tremendous sums allocated annually toward military and police, with the object of terrorizing populations of cities rather than housing them. We can channel those resources toward fixing those buildings that can be fixed and replacing those that cannot. Once the current public housing stock is refurbished, the next goal must be restarting public housing construction and siting these developments in locations that are desirable to working class communities.

Such a program would be expensive. But what is often neglected is that the US government already spends enormous amounts—roughly $200 billion annually—on housing, from mortgage deductions to developer tax breaks and private housing vouchers. Most of that spending goes to homeowners, including over $85 billion to households making over $100,000.[5] The rest is largely spent on private rental subsidies; just $7 billion goes to government owned and managed housing.[6] At the local level, most spending comes in the form of tax income ceded to private developers; the nearly $2.75 billion New York gives away in landlord and developer tax breaks every year is just one example.[7] The real estate state injects an enormous

---

5   Fischer, Will and Barbara Sard. "Chart book: Federal housing spending is poorly matched to need." Center on Budget and Policy Priorities, March 8, 2017.

6   Congressional Budget Office. *Federal housing assistance for low-income households*. September 2015.

7   New York City Department of Finance, Division of Tax Policy. *Annual Report on Tax Expenditures*. Fiscal Year 2017.

volume of capital for such inadequate results because we are subsidizing *capitalist* housing, which assumes a profit. As Esteban Girón of the Crown Heights Tenants Union argues, "If we want affordable housing, the city can build affordable housing. It doesn't have to be profitable by any stretch of the imagination."[8] A public option already exists. Public housing is not a dream, it is a reality that should be improved and expanded.

We can also rethink the relationship between real estate and taxes. Common municipal services, from schools and libraries to sidewalks and playgrounds, are primarily funded by property taxes. This leads to incredible service disparities between neighboring municipalities, corresponding directly to racist housing and labor practices. Today, taxes are one of the main ways real estate capital controls cities; if tax codes were reworked, they could be means by which cities control capital. Vacant apartments, buildings and land can be taxed to discourage warehousing and money laundering. Banks can be taxed heavily every time they foreclose on a home, dramatically changing the economic calculus of dispossession. A luxury fee can be charged to buyers of properties worth far more than the median rate, making such apartments less valuable for purchasers and therefore less likely to be produced. A similar tax can be placed on non-primary residences. Finally—and perhaps most importantly for the particular dilemma of planners in the real estate state—cities can tax away any increased revenue that landlords derive from public initiatives. In this

8   Siudzinski, Erica. "Crown Heights residents protest Bedford Armory site development." *Gothamist*, December 7, 2016.

scenario, the portion of profits a property owner generates from land itself—the value that comes from land's location, preparation, proximity to transit and public infrastructure connectivity—would be understood as socially produced and therefore no one's to own. A steep tax could expropriate that value and thus prevent landowners from profiting off the collective work of city making. This approach to land and taxation is at least as old as the nineteenth-century political economist Henry George—and therefore as old as the planning profession itself—but it remains relevant today.[9]

These proposals have all sought to readjust the balance between landlords and tenants, and real estate and the state. There's a whole other way for planners in a capitalist democracy to challenge real estate, though, and that's to bring back another competing element of capital. In addition to reining in real estate, planners can prioritize the reindustrialization of postindustrial, FIRE-economy cities. This would mean using zoning, tax policy, rent regulation and subsidies to keep existing industrial projects going, and invest heavily in the kinds of infrastructure—ports, energy, rails and more—industrial firms would need.

In this strategy, achieving industrial renewal is not just an economic development program, but also a strategy to combat real estate capital's monopoly on city planning priorities. Returning to Richard Foglesong's insights, planners in a diverse economy mitigate the demands from real estate capital (whose profitability depends on ever-rising real estate values) and those from industrial capital (whose profitability depends on

---

9 George, Henry. *Progress and poverty*. JM Dent, 1930 [1879].

low land values).[10] Planners in the real estate state have little incentive to do anything resulting in lower land values, but bringing back manufacturing could alter that calculus.

Reindustrialization might be a worthy way to diversify urban economies, but it comes with its own challenges. First, industrial capital would have to be heavily regulated in order to curb worker exploitation and environmental degradation. Second, real estate capitalists could find ways to profit from reindustrialization. In Brooklyn's Sunset Park, for example, global investors are pouring billions of dollars into "maker-space" projects like Industry City, which on the surface look like innovative industrial hubs but are in fact just a different form of rent-gouging real estate. Third, as long as there are other places with cheaper land and more suppressed labor, planners will struggle to lure manufacturers back to cities undergoing gentrification.

The other way to think about labor and land is to raise wages in the current employment sectors so that today's high rents have less of an impact on household budgets. For labor movements, that means vigorous organizing across all sectors, with a particular emphasis on those areas that can disrupt the everyday mechanisms of the global economy.[11] For planners, it means supporting a rising minimum wage, adopting pro-union policies and encouraging worker-owned cooperatives. This strategy would work as long as land and housing costs remain steady; however, if rents rise proportionate to wages,

---

10   Foglesong, *Planning the capitalist city: The colonial era to the 1920s.* Princeton University Press, 1986.

11   Moody, *On new terrain.*

as we would expect, landlords would expropriate all of labors' wage gains and workers would be left without any additional money in their pockets.

Ultimately, we cannot resolve the paradoxes of planning, land and labor with a different kind of capitalism.[12] We can alter the dynamics, tipping the scales toward the exploited and oppressed, but even the best-case scenario under these conditions would amount to a return to what Richard Foglesong described as the property contradiction and the capitalist-democracy contradiction: the principal purpose of capitalist planning is to balance the competing demands of capital against those of labor. To be sure, planners working within those contradictions have produced places of beauty, but they have also built an infrastructure of inequality. If we want to deal with the fundamental problems of capitalist urban planning, we have to move beyond the systems we are familiar with and fight for an anti-capitalist city.

Principles

In order to envision another urbanism, we need to establish a set of core principles: a political horizon, a set of benchmarks that guide our practice and a criteria for evaluating what sorts of demands help or hinder the realization of our goals.

A primary principle might be *public stewardship* over planning. In the capitalist context, this means more publicly managed infrastructure, from housing and hospitals to energy and rails,

---

12   Engels, Friedrich. *The housing question*. International publishers, 1935 [1872].

and it means more public access to urban space, from parks and plazas to streets and government buildings. Expanding access and ownership is important, but it is not enough.

True public stewardship would make space a public good. This may seem abstract, but it is as concrete and material as the shape of the city itself. It means democratizing planning so that workers and residents have the ultimate say over changes to the built environment, preservation or demolition of existing structures, provision of space to different uses and users, and modes of moving through the city. It means not just participating in a process organized by and for the propertied class, but seizing control of the means of spatial production.

This control can be leveraged through democratic government, popular assembly or some other form yet to be elaborated by our movements. In any manifestation, the animating spirit of these demands is that the people who produce space through their everyday labor and practice—and not just those with the money to buy a piece of land and property—should control its form and function: the city must belong to those who build it, not those who buy it.

Our movements should stress that the product of public stewardship would not just be a more democratic planning system, but also a more beautiful city. When urban space is a public good rather than a private right, city dwellers no longer have to decide between desirable features that might displace them (like attractive urban design or denser dwellings) and harmful threats that keep speculators away (like bad traffic and pollution). This is a choice no one should have to make; it is only the reign of property that forces working class communities to decide between beauty and stability. As workers have insisted for over one hundred years, we deserve not just bread, but roses too.

To realize public stewardship, we will need a second principle grounded in a radical shift in property relations: *socialized land*. As long as land and buildings are bought and sold in a private market, there can be no truly democratic control over the city. Capitalist cities are so structured around land and homeownership that it has come to seem entirely natural for property owners to hold enormous economic, legal, spatial, social and cultural advantages over all others, and for most of that privilege to be passed down as a form of inheritance. This logic runs deep through our cultures and societies. As the veteran New York housing organizer Wasim Lone once pointed out to me, even the language we use to describe this relationship is older than capitalism—land*lord*! A socialist city has no room for such feudal relations.

The principle, however, is easy to lose in the language. Socialism is all about the preservation of property—not the *private property* of commodities, but the *personal property* of one's body, labor and destiny. Marx closed Volume One of *Capital* with the declaration: "the capitalist mode of production and accumulation, and therefore capitalist private property as well, have for their fundamental condition the annihilation of that private property which rests on the labor of the individual himself; in other words, the expropriation of the worker."[13] The goal, then, is not abolishing property *per se*, but unmaking

---

13   Marx, Karl. *Capital: A critique of political economy, volume I*. Translated by Fowkes, Ben. Penguin, 1976 [1867], 940.

the social relations that produce capitalist private property. In terms of city planning, we are particularly concerned with turning land from commodity to commons.

Presently, commodified land is the norm throughout the country and much of the world. US land use regulations are exceptionally complicated, but, as David Harvey argues, property holders still "possess a class monopoly over land use."[14] Urban planners are above all land use managers, yet their power is subordinate to landowners—not just the individuals who own land and houses, but the organized power of real estate capital, in both its concentrated (billionaire developers) and diffuse (exclusionary homeowner associations) forms.

This power is more visible than ever under President Trump, and therefore perhaps more susceptible to concerted challenges. As Manissa Maharawal and Erin McElroy of the Bay Area's Anti-Eviction Mapping Project (AEMP) write:

> If we agree that racial justice and economic justice are bound up in each other, and that the history of private property in the United States is one of dispossession, colonialism and structural racism, if we understand the political moment in the United States as one in which a racist landlord has just taken power and empowered others like him, then we at the AEMP say that it is time for the housing movement to move beyond reformist argument and demand the abolition of private property.[15]

---

14   Harvey, David. *Social justice and the city*. Blackwell, 1973, 179.
15   Maharawal, Manissa and Erin McElroy (The Anti Eviction Mapping Project). "In the time of Trump: Housing, whiteness and abolition." *Abolition:*

Land must no longer be translatable into a dollar count. Homes must not be traded on open markets, and transposed into fictitious capital through speculation and securitization. Publicly owned land and buildings must not be treated as budgetary burdens or bargaining chips in deals with developers, but rather as the precursor to a decommodified urban future. In Rob Robinson's vision, "if land was used for common good as opposed to commodity, we could grow food, and we could build shelter, we could self-govern ourselves. With our lives more stable, we could find education and good medical care. Land represents stability in one's life."[16]

Socialized land may seem like a faraway vision, but its outlines are already here. Public space, from parks, sidewalks and community gardens to public housing, lending libraries and municipal buildings, are everyday aspects of urban life and provide spaces of beauty and social reproduction in the heart of the city. Between government and nonprofit facilities, parks and streets, well over half of New York City's land mass is already outside the purely private domain. Ninety miles from Miami, Cuban land and housing are almost entirely public— every household has a home, but until recently no one owned them. In China, land is largely owned by the state, which offers long-term leases to private building owners. The same is true in state-capitalist Singapore, where over 80 percent of residents from all classes live in public housing. These programs are a far

16   Robinson, Rob. From the interview series, "Balm in Gilead: Stories from Black organizers." nyf.org/balm-in-gilead/rob-robinson

cry from the utopian, but they demonstrate that some cities already function without private land ownership.

There are many scales and means through which this principle can be applied. Public housing can be expanded into currently private buildings, thus socializing housing on a rolling basis. Alternately, land can be socialized before buildings are expropriated, leaving housing private but preventing land speculation. Or, in a truly revolutionary scenario, the whole city can be expropriated and redistributed. In all of these cases, at any scale, the relationship between real estate and planning is not just adjusted but exploded.

Putting land in the public domain would require a whole lot of coordination and planning. In order to democratically manage all that public land, we will need a third principle: *a reordered regionalism.* Planners of all political stripes extol regionalism, though their visions are entirely different. Liberals like those at the Brookings Institution's Metropolitan Policy Program envision shared services across cities and suburbs as a way of redistributing resources without redistributing income. Conservatives coming out of the "public choice" school of planning argue that regions should specialize in particular economic sectors and workers should move across them in order to find the best fit.

Radicals, including nearly every planner I talked with, are drawn to regionalism because it subverts political boundaries. Social democrats like the early to mid-twentieth-century Regional Planning Association of America viewed regionalism as key to eliminating both urban and rural exploitation. Anarchists like Kropotkin saw in regionalism a more organic alternative to the arbitrary and violent rule of national governments.

Given its disparate supporters, it's clear that regionalism holds a range of meanings, and does not by itself suggest anything particularly liberating. What regionalism does, however, is free us to consider the geographical scales at which we want to plan the various elements of society, rather than rely on the existing (and often clumsy) units of districts, cities, states and countries. It also provides a way out of the deeply conservative norm of devolution—"the name for structural adjustment in richer, inequality-riven politics," Ruth Wilson Gilmore and Craig Gilmore argue.[17] Devolution manifests in the form of a contradiction: the simultaneous *dispersal* of responsibility for public functions to local governments and *centralization* of control over funding and priorities at the federal level. It leads to awful outcomes, like a public housing system whose supply and funding is restricted by the federal government but whose maintenance and management is assumed by chronically underfunded local authorities. Radical regionalism helps break down the arbitrary but normalized political boundaries that have captured and confined our political imaginaries.

The kind of regionalism that most radical planners embrace today is a complex one, operating simultaneously at multiple scales, from the hyper-local to the global. The key is matching planning functions with the geographical scale that is a) the best ecological fit; and b) the most likely to resist capitalist

---

17   Gilmore, Ruth Wilson and Craig Gilmore. "Beyond Bratton." In Camp, Jordan T. and Christina Heatherton (eds). *Policing the planet: Why the policing crisis led to Black Lives Matter*. Verso Books, 2016, 188.

control. Large-scale planning can be effective at overcoming local economic and political fiefdoms. As Robert Fitch wrote, "The aim of the Right is always to restrict the scope of class conflict—to bring it down to as low a level as possible. The smaller and more local the political unit, the easier it is to run it oligarchically."[18] National and international planning, however, can also trounce local opposition and subvert working class community control. What is needed is a complex and flexible regionalism, one which starts at the scale most appropriate for a given planning function but can be taken over from above or below if plans are being shaped toward the demands of a powerful elite.

This requires democratic and responsive planning at all levels: not a privileged professional class of experts overseeing an otherwise egalitarian state, but a society in which people plan and control their spaces at all scales. The Soviet system claimed to be a perfectly planned workers' state, but, as socialist scholar Hal Draper argued, its top-down centralized nature ensured this could never be the case. Draper wrote in 1963, "the separation of planning from democratic control-from-below makes a mockery of planning itself; for the immensely complicated industrial societies of today cannot be effectively planned by an all-powerful central committee's *ukases*, which inhibit and terrorize the free play of initiative and correction from below."[19] The only way to really plan, then, is through

---

18　Fitch, Robert. "What is union democracy?" *New Politics*, XIII-2.50, Winter 2011.

19　Draper, Hal. *The two souls of socialism: Socialism from below v. socialism from above.* Young People's Socialist League, 1963. "Ukases" roughly

popular control: of workplaces and buildings, as well as of cities and regions.

Reordered regionalism, socialized land and public steward-ship are big ideas, and, admittedly, kind of sketchy. But they are not outlandish, and they are certainly not novel. In fact, most of them have been around for centuries. The question, at least for this country, is why these ideas are still dreams and not realities. For capitalist cities like New York, and in capi-talist countries like the United States, the problem has never been a lack of good alternatives, but rather a political climate that never allowed them to take hold.

Politics

When planners think about their work, they often describe a box full of tools—particular approaches to space that can be used at the appropriate time and place. For many plan-ners, then, change means picking up a different tool than they would otherwise grab, or developing new tools to work on new problems. Like hammers and saws, planning tools can be powerful but dangerous—someone else can always pick them up and use them against us. Policies are stronger, but they can be reversed by incoming administrations. Laws are even more durable, but they too can be undone.

In order to really work differently, planners need structural changes in the urban political economy. The only way those come about is as a result of large, disruptive mass movements,

translates into English as "edicts."

organized not only to make demands of the state but also to make the status quo untenable. Planners will follow, but they cannot lead. Urban movements, then, must have a planning vision, and better yet a plan.

At first glance, this might seem like a tough time for movements to fight gentrification, decommodify land and rethink planning. They have a mighty enemy in modern financialized real estate, which not only dominates the urban landscape but the global circuits of capital investment. So far, major victories have been few and far between. The real estate state, however, has considerable vulnerabilities.

Where manufacturing capital dominates, the industrial workplace becomes a main site of struggle and the union movement the leading voice of labor. Where real estate is the dominant sect of capital, however, the importance of a strong and dedicated housing, tenant and anti-gentrification movement increases and becomes a crucial conduit for labor action. This is not to say that workplace struggles matter any less in places where real estate rules—deindustrialization simply means working for a different form of capital, not ceasing to work and be exploited. But just as a globalized economy means that workers at particular logistical chokepoints can effectively shut down the entire system with targeted strikes, an urban economy overdependent on real estate means that a large and effective tenant movement has the power to deny speculators the chance to use the city as an investment vehicle.

Anti-gentrification movements can therefore develop a transformative platform of anti-capitalist struggle alongside movements focused on the workplace. In fact, success in housing movements can create more opportunities for mobilizations elsewhere. As Lisa Ortega of Take Back the Bronx explains, "people begin to organize more once they have a place to lay their head."[20] Conversely, workplace organizing can feed into fights over planning and gentrification. According to David Tieu of the National Mobilization Against Sweatshops, which organizes against both workplace exploitation and planned gentrification in Chinatown and the Lower East Side, "people began to realize that it's not enough just to fight in the workplace, for small economic gains, but to see how the economic struggle connects to the struggles of the community, to fight for greater control of what's going on."[21]

Shop floor production certainly holds a central place in the capitalist system, but it is far from the only site of exploitation. Production must be joined by distribution, realization, consumption and social reproduction in order for the entire system to work. Effective social movements target all aspects of the capitalist value chain, but most tend to focus their energies on a particular element. Union fights usually take place at the point of production; transportation struggles contest distribution; boycotts target consumption; welfare movements are fought on the terrain of social reproduction. Housing movements are social reproduction struggles too, and are often linked to questions of production, distribution and consumption, but their power can be harnessed through their ability to

20   Anderson, Stefan and Rahima Nasa. "Bronxites march to reject Trump." *Mott Haven Herald*, November 28, 2016.

21   Lim, Audrea. "Chinatown resistance: The struggle against rezoning and gentrification in Lower Manhattan." *Brooklyn Rail*, February 4, 2009.

threaten realization: the point at which people's hard-earned pay is handed over to their landlord, so that the landlord can turn a profit on their investment. If tenants don't pay up, property capitalists are thrown into crisis. A true landlord crisis in the real estate state could create the conditions for radical and widespread change.

Mass rent strikes, eviction blockades and anti-foreclosure occupations all do this, and are all bubbling up in cities around the world.[22] Likewise with campaigns that freeze out luxury developers and promote public or non-commoditized housing alternatives. Laws that severely limit private rent increases can also throw a wrench in the system, since speculative landlords can only repay their debts if rents rise rapidly.

The key is to re-center rent as a political issue. In New York, the political system is set up to occlude rent from political discussion, with the exception of a few designated venues in opaque corners of civic life: the dysfunctional state capital when the rent regulations periodically sunset, and the mayoral-appointed Rent Guidelines Board that sets new rent levels each summer. Despite this sidelining, long-standing tenant unions, as well as newer ad hoc collectives, constantly engage in unsung organizing against rent hikes and landlord harassment. These groups are fighting not only for a more affordable city, but also to make these life and death matters legible as politics.

---

22   Lang, Marissa J. "Rent strikes grow in popularity among tenants as gentrification drives up rents in cities like D.C." *Washington Post*, June 9, 2018; Roy, Ananya. "Dis/possessive collectivism: Property and personhood at city's end." *Geoforum* 80 (2017): A1–11.

More commonly, however, housing politics is reduced to the issue of density. New York, like many cities, has an extensive public process for changing building densities through zoning. Whenever a change is proposed to the legal framework that governs how much can be built where, there is a mandatory review that involves a great deal of study, debate, and often protest. Proponents of greater construction can be relied on to tout the potential benefits of ever-upward densities, which are said to create myriad economic and ecological efficiencies as well as social and aesthetic opportunities. There are certainly scenarios in which that is true, but this simplistic framework elides the fact that most of what is constructed post-upzoning is aimed toward the very top of the real estate market, and does nothing to alleviate costs for most residents. In human terms, that kind of luxury construction does not even guarantee greater numbers of people living in a given area; in fact, in some scenarios it can reduce, rather than expand, urban densities. While upscale developments may contain more "units" than their older, more affordable precursors, they are often "filled" with shell investors, single-person households and large footprinted retail, thus reducing the number of people within an area and belying the supposed environmental, economic and social benefits of density for density's sake. Those arguments, then, hold little appeal to urban residents seeking to prevent their own displacement.

While the size and shape of new buildings certainly matter to neighborhood residents, the most threatening aspect of a change in allowable density is generally its potential to alter the exchange value of land. The changing price of land and resulting increases in rents, however, are not factors most land use systems are adept at calculating or considering. Because of these narrowing political opportunities, savvy activists use density as a proxy for the more basic issue of rent, and frame their campaigns around questions like: if more is built here, will neighboring housing costs rise? If we prevent big new construction projects, can we keep housing costs low?

Such campaigns are important means to confront new-build gentrification and contest the luxury makeover of our cities, but they can sometimes get mired in the alienating abstractions and esoteric minutia of land use regulation—floor area ratios, sky exposure planes or the relative merits of an R7D versus C6-2A zoning designation. In order to stay focused on the issues that matter most, such campaigns must be bolstered by a strong, radical and organized tenant movement. Tenant movements are uniquely capable of grounding the abstraction of "housing" in the lived reality of home. They focus on present as well as future threats, and take decisive aim at the forces that feed on working class communities every month of the year.

In many cities, tenants could form an unbeatable bloc. At 68 percent of New York City residents, tenants compose a larger fraction of the population than almost any other demographic unit: any gender, any religion, any racial grouping (including all people of color combined) or either immigrants or US-born residents.[23] The source of tenants' potential power,

---

23   US Census Bureau. American Community Survey, 2016 (5-Year Estimates); Jones, Robert P. *Religion in New York City's Five Boroughs.* Purdue Policy Research Institute, April 13, 2016.

however, is not just their numbers or their structurally significant position within the global value chain, though both of those are crucial factors. As political philosopher and South Bronx Unite co-founder Monxo López argues, the force that motivates tenant movements is their intrinsic relationship to land and home, a personal and collective subjectivity that can transform residents into a formidable force of resistance. This relationship between people and places can also take reactionary forms, from exclusionary communitarianism to "blood and soil" nationalism; this, however, is not a reason to abandon affective politics around specific locations, but rather a reason to struggle over its meaning.

In New York, there is growing momentum around the activist slogan "Not For Sale." It is chanted at rallies and plastered over posters for posh new developments. In early 2016, a network of activists called "New York City Not for Sale" released a five-point platform that is, ultimately, a radical anti-gentrification plan:

1. *End homelessness in New York City.* Immediate housing for all homeless people through new construction or seizure of vacant "warehoused" properties. Citywide moratorium on evictions.

2. *Universal rent control.* Apply rent control laws to all rental properties in New York City. Institute an immediate rent freeze, and phased rollback of rents to 20 percent of tenant income.

3. *Transfer distressed buildings to tenant ownership.* Transfer properties using the 7A receivership process or eminent domain. Tenant ownership in the form of cooperatives, mutual housing associations, or community land trusts.

4. *Repair and expand high-quality public housing.* Full funding for the NYC Housing Authority (NYCHA) and full repairs and enhancements for all NYCHA properties. Begin construction of new, high quality public housing with community centers and art spaces.

5. *Democratize development.* Institute direct election of community boards with veto power over development decisions. Expand public input into the Uniform Land Use Review Procedure (ULURP). Moratorium on upzoning until these reforms are completed.[24]

This is a plan to transition from the system we have to the one we might want. None of the five points are yet visible on the current political horizon, but nor are they complete hallucinations. They take what we have now—such as programs to combat homelessness, limited rent control, ways of wresting buildings from bad landlords, faulty public housing and community consultation—and turn them into something bolder, more democratic and less profit-oriented.

Mainstream housing groups scoff at this kind of program. They see it as a waste of time—why bother demanding the

---

24   NYC Not For Sale Network, nycnot4sale.org.

impossible? But New York City Not For Sale's plan does something more subversive than that. Because it builds its alternatives around what already exists, it shows city residents how much better urban life could be without necessarily inventing a new city from whole cloth.

This vision mirrors the experience of many visitors to Havana. One of the most shocking realizations upon arrival is that nearly the entire city is in the public domain. This is jolting not only because our cities are so private, but because revolutionary Havana remains the same old city, built by slaves and wageworkers for colonial exploitation long before its expropriation by the revolutionary government. While there are a few new buildings in the center and some Soviet-style housing developments on the periphery, the vast majority of the old city stands, with its mansions, tree-lined boulevards and walled waterfront. The revolution did not blow up the colonial city; it took it, retained the beauty it created and transformed the social relations that had produced it.

This is how we need to think about radical change in our own cities. New Yorkers, like anyone else, are deeply attached to their homes, their blocks and their neighborhoods, even while the cost of living there infuriates them. They love the city, but they hate it too. Plans like New York City Not For Sale's help residents see how they could build on what they hold dear while tearing down what oppresses them.

The pivot toward socialized planning can begin on multiple fronts, including challenging the way people perceive what surrounds them today and imagine what is possible for the future. Long before structural transformations take hold, radical planners and social movements can pursue demonstration projects—small-scale programs that model alternative modes of development and can alter people's consciousness about what is a possible, and even what is preferable. Such experimental alternatives will not change the fundamentals of the capitalist system, but they can inspire participation in political struggles toward those higher goals. Model projects were an important component of early US public and subsidized housing programs, with "modern housing" developments rising during the early days of the New Deal to demonstrate that other ways of building and living were not only doable but desirable.

Highlighting the ways cities already reclaim space for common use, such as when planners take car-clogged streets and turn them into pedestrian walkways, can also be a useful way to open people's eyes to more radical possibilities. Of course, in the current system, the benefits of these projects are mostly accrued by nearby landowners; if we just build pedestrian plazas and leave it at that, we do little more than add value to landlords' portfolios. But if we use the plaza to demonstrate the principle, we can show that space is regularly reappropriated in ways that once seemed impossible.

While we highlight the positive possibilities, planners and social movements need to be more assertive in showing what goes wrong when elements of life we are used to being public are suddenly turned private. Right now, for example, private equity firms are buying up public water systems in poor cities and making a killing off the deals. Trump's infrastructure plans would magnify this practice manifold. The point of exposing these horrors is not just to turn back the tide on privatization, but also to show people that the systems they've always known as private commodities might actually work better in the public domain. Water in the public domain is a fairly common notion; housing in the public domain, however, takes some more creative thought. But in order for that thought to occur, people need to see how much better public services can be than their profit-oriented alternatives.

Similarly, public actions that reclaim space can change popular opinion about the city that surrounds them. Occupy Wall Street turned one of New York's many mundane privately owned public spaces (POPS) into the single liveliest and genuinely public space in the city for several months. After taking that space, protesters felt emboldened to look elsewhere, temporarily liberating other POPS, parks and even fully private spaces, and confronting the police who tried to stop them. More recently, Black Lives Matter has inspired people to reclaim urban spaces of all sorts—including sites of police murder, symbolically important spaces of state power and logistical chokepoints in the heart of the city—as part of confrontational protests against state violence. By shunning the long-standing but politically nullifying protest norms of police permitting and pre-negotiated civil disobedience, both Black Lives Matter and Occupy Wall Street have emboldened urban residents to not just take *to* the streets, but to *take* the streets, for marches, memorials and encampments. These kinds of actions, though sporadic in nature, open people's eyes to the possibility of a more public city.

In a quieter but no less profound way, genuine and democratic community planning initiatives—independent undertakings that encourage people to come together and create comprehensive plans for their neighborhoods—can change the way people think about the relationship between themselves, their neighbors, their landlords and their government. Marie Kennedy calls this "transformative community planning" because at its best, the process of planning—not just the plan's implementation—can begin to alter these social relations.[25]

At its worst, however, it can lead working class communities down a fruitless path of endless meetings with few results. This was planner-turned-critic Frances Fox Piven's appraisal of the advocacy planning model, which, she argued in 1970, did more to reinforce inequalities than it did to challenge them:

> [I]nvolving local groups in elaborate planning procedures is to guide them into a narrowly circumscribed form of political action, and precisely that form for which they are least equipped. What is laid out for the poor when their advocate arrives is a strategy of political participation which, to be effective, requires powerful group support, stable organization, professional staff, and money—precisely those resources which the poor do not have ... The absorbing and elaborate planning procedures which follow may be effective in dampening any impulse toward disruptive action which has always been the main political recourse of the very poor.[26]

---

25   Kennedy, Marie. "Transformative community planning: Empowerment through community development." *New Solutions: A Journal of Environmental and Occupational Health Policy* 6.4 (1997): 93–100.

26   Piven, "Whom does the advocate planner serve?", 35.

What, then, is the difference between meaningful community-based planning and meaningless participatory co-optation? In short, good community planning builds power for those shut out of the formal planning process, allows them to elaborate a vision that stands in contrast to that of the real estate state, and clarifies who and what stands between their demand and its implementation. In some cases, disparate groups will come to a consensus and develop a winning campaign around that change. More often than not, however, different factions will form and fight over opposing visions of community development.

This looks like failure to most planners and nonprofit organizers, who are usually trained to work through or eschew these kinds of conflicts and seek solutions that bridge divides within communities. But sharpening these contradictions should be one of the most important functions of community planning. There is no way to plan for everyone. It's not exactly a zero-sum game—it's much more complicated than that— but there is no such thing as a universal solution. Landlords and tenants do not want the same urban planning, just like bosses and workers do not want the same salary structures. Radicals engaged in community-based planning must not bureaucratically manage class conflict, but rather accentuate it. A rowdy community planning process can help those excluded from the formal system develop a counter-vision and organize around it.

For decades, municipalities have regularly hosted participatory planning sessions where residents are invited to play with maps of their neighborhood and tell planners where they want things like bus stops and libraries to go. There's nothing wrong with this in principle, but, as geographer John Carr—who observed these games as a member of a task force on skate park planning in Seattle—notes, even more elaborately participatory processes tend to "render political decisions apparently apolitical." The process "enables political elites—including elected officials, effective advocacy organizations, businesses, and well-organized neighborhood groups—to reframe their policy preferences as the product of ground-level democratic processes, and open, fair, and impartial technocratic decision-making."[27]

Today, more and more community organizers are boycotting participatory planning sessions altogether, refusing to give cover to processes designed to make them feel good about losing. The Experimental Nucleus of Conflictual Planning in Rio de Janeiro, Brazil, for example, trains communities to view capitalist urban planning as an inherently conflict-based—not a consensus-driven—process, in which the only way to productively participate is to forcefully assert collective demands while refusing to cooperate in projects based in dispossession or displacement. As urban residents around the world become more familiar with the tools of real estate rule, such sentiments and strategies may become increasingly common and powerful.

---

27 Carr, John. "Making urban politics go away: The role of legally mandated planning processes in occluding city power." In Davidson and Martin (eds). *Urban Politics*, 112–13.

Consciousness and Contradictions

All consciousness is contradictory, but the situation for
capitalist urban planners is especially thorny. They are simultaneously far-seeing visionaries and day-to-day pragmatists.
They are asked to imagine new systems, but tasked with
operating old ones. They must simultaneously represent the
interests of those they plan for and those who hire them. They
are perceived both as individuals with agency and instru-
ments of their governments. Their work is situated in the
future, but must address the public in the present while taking heed of history.

Finally, and most profoundly, they conduct public planning in a private land market. Under real estate's rule, their
job at best is to create social benefits that private interests will
ultimately usurp. At worst, they create private benefits and
pitch them to the public. Capitalist planners are therefore in
the impossible position of representing both real estate capital
and those most threatened by it.

While these are deep contradictions, they are certainly not
eternal. In fact, under the right circumstances, they present
radical openings—a chance not only for planners to reimagine their work, but for all of us to likewise reimagine planning.
Over the years, the capitalist system has proven astoundingly
resistant to crisis after crisis; we should never assume that the
weight of its own contradictions, or those of its planners in particular, will be enough to bring it down for good. The rise of
the real estate state, which paradoxically sank money into land
at the same time as global capital was becoming increasingly

footloose, is evidence of this resiliency. If we want to explode the contradictions that wrack contemporary capitalist urban planning, we have to change not only the planners but also the political context in which they work.

For radical planners in public office, the leading task is to get organized: find each other, meet outside of work, share information, introduce each other to new ideas and keep each other honest. Organizing can help combat the groupthink and bureaucratic fatalism that often takes hold within city agencies, and remind radical planners that while they may be alone in their workplace, they are not alone in their workforce.

There are a number of past examples of such organizing. From 1967 to 1974, members of Movement for a Democratic Society formed the Urban Underground, which organized planners—primarily in New York's Department of City Planning—to study radical texts, demonstrate, testify and publish critiques of city plans. From 1964 to 1972, Planners for Equal Opportunity brought together planners whose work supported the civil rights and Black Power movements, and aimed to act as a national counterweight to the mainstream American Institute of Planners (now the American Planning Association). During those same years, Student Nonviolent Coordinating Committee members formed the Architects' Renewal Committee of Harlem, which brought planners, architects and designers together with neighborhood residents to plot the spatial specifics of Black self-determination. From 1975 to the present, Planners Network has connected radical planners and urban organizers through its meetings, newsletters, publications and conferences.

Since most big city planning departments are part of larger municipal labor organizations, the union might be a secure home for such activity, as long as local leadership can be either grasped or evaded. This would not only bring people together, but also provide some job protections for those engaged in riskier political activity. In order to stave off isolation and foster creative action, radical planners need to build an active organizing culture that can both incubate new ideas and expand their ranks.

All of this presumes a major break with politics as usual. After all, most cities are quickly moving in diametrically opposed directions. Turning radical ideas into reality will require robust and organized movements. Constrained by the perverse incentives of the capitalist state, as well as their limited power, planners alone lack the means to enact this program without higher state authority, and real estate-aligned politicians will not be inclined to try these actions without forceful protest and challenges from the public. We can and should be mad at planners, but ultimately they cannot undo real estate's grasp over the city until people wrest back power from those who profit off land.

Conclusion

Cities seem to be heading in two different directions at once.

Some places are bursting with capital, largely channeled through land and property investment. These hyper-invested cities are becoming more expensive and attracting higher income dwellers, even as they continue to depend on low-wage workers. Displacement is becoming a regular occurrence and a constant fear for working class residents.

Other places are facing disinvestment, with employment declining, housing falling into dangerous disrepair and vulture capitalists stalking the streets in search of assets to strip. Their city leaders are scrambling for cash and trying anything to get investors' attention, including selling off public land, slashing taxes and investing in "creative city" features. Here, the trend has shifted from "smokestack chasing" to "skyscraper chasing"—two races to the bottom, in which cities and states compete for capital investment by offering low taxes, lax regulation and disciplined labor.

Hyper-investment and extreme disinvestment seem like separate, parallel, one-way streets that cities travel down toward opposite futures. These contrasting tendencies, however, are closer than they appear.

First, hyper-invested and deeply disinvested cities are not necessarily separate places. Often they coexist within the same municipality, and even on the same block. Cities like Newark and Chicago are simultaneously expanding and collapsing in value. Even in extreme examples, the opposite is always present. Los Angeles is home to some of the world's wealthiest individuals, as well as tens of thousands of people who live on the streets and in shelters. Some paint Baltimore as emblematic of urban crisis, but there too exist pockets of great wealth. Urban inequality is not so much a question of rich cities and poor cities, as the simultaneous and dependent relationship of wealth and poverty.

Second, these two urban futures tilt toward each other. One person's disinvestment is another's deal, as abandoned properties and vacant lots are purchased on the cheap, reinvested, redeveloped and resold for enormous profits. At the same time, overinvested places are vulnerable to surplus crises—too much investment in properties no one will buy or rent—and when the bubble bursts, the rents and sale prices fall. Each process can be a precondition for the other.

Finally, these urban divergences are expressions of the same phenomenon: a political economy organized around real estate. When space becomes the primary commodity and rents overdetermine all other economic activity, cities become vulnerable to extremes of wealth and poverty, glitz and grit. Everyone plays their part: financiers make derivatives that spin housing into abstractions; architects make boxes for high-end investment; politicians make promises to build, build, build; and planners bend space toward profit.

These characteristics of the real estate state are easiest to spot in expensive cities like New York, where landlords and developers effectively control the political machine and planning apparatus, but they are just as present in cheaper cities like Las Vegas, where subprime mortgages burned through the landscape like wildfire. Geographer Patrick Vitale argues that Pittsburgh and Detroit, two rust belt cities frequently portrayed respectively as models of postindustrial success and failure, are actually experiencing inverse versions of the same phenomenon. "The Pittsburgh region can be likened to Detroit—the most-cited example of urban decline—but turned inside out. In Michigan, capital fled to the suburbs, leaving behind a crumbling city center. In Pennsylvania, deindustrialization decimated Pittsburgh's suburbs, while some parts of the city enjoyed relatively stable investment."[1] Whether the money is going into or out of cities, capital's relation to land is the guiding force in these regions' trajectories.

All of these places link their destinies to rising property values and set their planners to work finding clever ways to accomplish that goal above all others. Even when well-intentioned planners are not thinking about property values and instead aim to make space more beautiful and friendly for

---

1 Vitale, Patrick. "The Pittsburgh fairy tale." *Jacobin*, June 20, 2017.

working class residents, their efforts are usurped by landowners, who then raise the cost of living for the very people planners intended to serve.

When this planning model works, the result is gentrification: investors sweep in, property values rise and the people who suffered most from disinvestment are swept away by real estate's rising tide. The initial capital for reinvestment often comes directly out of other spaces, contributing to somewhere else's disinvestment and sending their planners on a mission to retrieve lost revenues.

Where gentrification takes hold, the city turns to neoliberal boosterism and treats public space as a private investment opportunity. Where gentrification fails, the city turns to neoliberal austerity and slashes the budgets for everything but the police. Because gentrification and disinvestment often occur simultaneously in the same cities, most governments and planning departments operate with a combination of both approaches.

Looking at this state of affairs, it would be easy to conclude that planners are the problem. On the right, libertarians see urban land crises and claim that government, not real estate capital, is to blame. They say that zoning codes artificially limit the housing stock, and that planners should get out of the way and let developers do their jobs. In this corporate paradise, "the market"—a euphemism for rich people—decides exactly what and who will go where. The vast majority of people will be excluded from that process and will have to use their meager market power to ensure their own survival. This kind of planning-by-not-planning ensures that the ruling class will continue to rule, and make a nice profit doing so.

There is less of an institutionalized anti-planning bias on the left, but there remains a generalized tendency toward do-it-ourselves hyper-localism, which rejects big government planning and delegates all decisions to the community level. Like the "unschoolers" who reject brick-and-mortar schools as inherently authoritarian, this voluntarist tradition views urban planning as an institution so thoroughly corrupted by capitalism that it ought to be abolished, or at least avoided. While libertarians treat planners as government stooges, left localists treat them as corporate lackeys.

Such vague appeals to community can be an abdication of reality rather than a political position. Community planning is a real and valuable practice, but it is about building power and forging coalitions within and beyond geographical boundaries; it is certainly not about finding the consensus solution to everyone's problems. Community control is itself a struggle, not just something to struggle for.

Rejecting communal absolutism, however, does not mean switching to its opposite and promoting strictly hierarchical, centralized planning. Just as the pure and harmonious community is a myth, so too is the all-seeing administrative state. Believing any one central power can reasonably and benevolently plan for all its residents is another way of rejecting politics by assuming that there are simple solutions to social problems.

Changing the scale of planning will never change the fact that planning is *always* political and never just a bureaucratic or technical exercise. Certain futures will be promoted while others are foreclosed. The rich and the poor will not share

equally, and racial and gender divisions will be either disman-
tled or maintained. Things will get built or they won't, and they
will go somewhere or other. These are all political decisions,
ones we cannot shy away from. Contentious planning is the
way we fight to "secure the future" we desire.[2] We need more
planning, not less, and we need to engage with the politics of
planning in order to change the way our cities work.

The contemporary politics of planning are stacked against
working class people, but that need not be the case. The planner's job is to turn social demands into physical space; whose
demands they follow depends entirely on whose command they
obey. In the United States and many other countries, they are
commanded by politicians who follow real estate's demands.
This, however, is no immutable law.

In this moment, planners are hugely important to the capitalist project of urban real estate investment. Through complex
schemes and accidental overtures, they develop the conditions
that attract investment and ensure its profitability. Our challenge is to recognize this fact without rejecting planning as
such, or wishing away its politics. While planning is surely
a tool of the powerful, it is also essential part of any strategy
to challenge them.

---

2   Gilmore, *Golden gulag*, 175.

Acknowledgments

I dedicate this work to my dad, Josh Stein, who was a great father, husband, historian, teacher, organizer and storyteller. He was too much of a materialist to believe in the afterlife, so I will not pretend I am writing to him now. I am writing to you, my reader, and all I can say is that if you never got to know him, you missed out. I thank him for everything he did for me and my brothers.

While the book is dedicated to my dad, it was my living family and friends who supported me while I wrote it. In particular, my wife, Sarah Friedland, was a constant inspiration, and my mother, Penney Stein, was a steadfast supporter. Many, many friends talked through the ideas in this book, and helped me find the words to express them—I cannot name them all, but I am thankful for every one of them. Special thanks to Oksana Mironova, who read and provided feedback on the entire manuscript, and Joel Feingold, Sarah Friedland, Ruth Wilson Gilmore, Manissa Maharawal and Hilary Wilson, who read and offered constructive critiques on chapters or sections in progress.

Thanks to the New York City housing movement, and to the tenant leaders who helped me think through the ideas in this book. Special thanks to the members, staff and board of Tenants & Neighbors, who taught me the finer points of New York housing policy and politics.

Dozens of teachers exposed me to the theories and histories that informed this work. Though some might disagree with my conclusions, I hope they will accept my gratitude. In college, I was inspired by Rachel Cohen, Eri Fujieda, María Elena García, Dean Hubbard, Jamee Moudud, Joshua Muldavin, Raymond Seidelman, Monica Varsanyi and Elke Zuern. In planning school, I learned from Tom Angotti, Ralph Blessing, John Chin, Alyssa Katz, Peter Kwong, Scott Larson, Kathryn Leek, Susan Turner Meiklejohn, William Milczarski, Stanley Moses, Ted Orosz, Laxmi Ramasubramanian and Sigmund Shipp. While pursuing my PhD in geography, I've had the honor of studying with Stanley Aronowitz, James Biles, Harold Connolly, Ruth Wilson Gilmore, Leigh Graham, James Jasper, Setha Low, Ruth Milkman and Marianna Pavlovskaya.

Sadly, several of these teachers will not be able to read these words. The great Ray Seidelman died in 2007, but I think of him often—these strange days especially. His course "Is the US a Democracy?", which began on September 11, 2001, laid out many of the questions considered here. Both Peter Kwong and Stanley Moses died suddenly while I was writing this book. Stanley taught me a great deal about regional inequality and the power of budgets, and strongly encouraged my intellectual and political pursuits. Peter was one of my closest mentors and greatest influences, and his intellectual fingerprints are scattered throughout these pages. Parts of Chapters 2 and 3 come from a project we started on gentrification in Chinatown. I cannot thank him enough for his generosity and inspiration.

Thanks too to all the teachers who never had me in their classrooms but nonetheless devoted countless hours to mentoring me, including Eve Baron, James DeFilippis, Tarry Hum, Aseem Inam, Cindi Katz, John Krinsky, Ian MacDonald, Peter Marcuse, Rob Robinson and Arturo Ignacio Sánchez.

I am grateful for all my students at Hunter, John Jay, the Murphy Institute, Parsons and Sarah Lawrence, who challenged my thinking on urban planning and geography. Thanks especially to Tenn Joe Lim, whose classroom comment during a discussion of Foglesong's *Planning the Capitalist City* helped inspire the last section of Chapter 1.

As I was editing the book, I appreciated the opportunity to share excerpts in various settings, including the American Association of Geographers, Association of Collegiate Schools of Planning, Historical Materialism, LaGuardia Urban Studies, New Brooklyn-Queens Waterfront and Spaces of Struggle conferences.

This book would not have been possible without the support and encouragement of Bhaskar Sunkara, publisher of *Jacobin Magazine*, and Ben Mabie, Andrew Hsiao, Duncan Ranslem, Jenn Harris and Wes House, my editors and publicist at Verso. Thanks to Benjamin Koditschek for contributing his talent toward the book's cover and design. A few passages from Chapters 3 and 4 first appeared in articles published in *Jacobin*.

Finally, thanks to the anonymous planners who shared their ideas about the way things are and the way they could be. Your secret identities are safe with me.